Painting Civil War Miniatures

Mike Davidson

Schiffer Publishing Ltd
77 Lower Valley Road, Atglen, PA 19310

Dedication

To my brothers Gary, Mark, Doug and Phil

Acknowledgements

The figure used in this book was produced by Michael-Roberts Ltd. For a complete catalog of this and other figures offered, contact:

Michael-Roberts Ltd.
2221 Hunters Road, SW
Roanoke, VA 24015
(703)343-2241

Contents

BOOK DESIGN BY AUDREY L. WHITESIDE.

Printed in China

ISBN: 0-88740-884-2

Library of Congress Cataloging-in-Publication Data

Davidson, Mike.
Painting Civil War miniatures / Mike Davidson.
p. cm.
ISBN 0-88740-884-2
1. Miniature craft. 2. Military miniatures--United States. 3. Miniature painting--Technique.
I. Title.
TT178.D3827 1995
745.592'82--dc20 95-24293
CIP

Published by Schiffer Publishing, Ltd.
77 Lower Valley Road
Atglen, PA 19310
Please write for a free catalog.
This book may be purchased from the publisher.
Please include $2.95 postage.
Try your bookstore first.

We are interested in hearing from authors with book ideas on related subjects.

Introduction

The painting of American Civil War figures is not a new hobby. Union troops and their Confederate brethren have emerged from the painter's hobby room for many years. In the past, many of these figures have been somewhat stiff and toy-like, devoid of detail and realism.

Today, things are quite different. The painter has a huge variety of excellent Civil War figure kits from which to choose. From the pomp and splendor of the Zouave uniform to the simple drab monotone of Confederate Butternut, the painter of Civil War figures has many color options from which to choose. The uniform colors provided at the end of this book may be adjusted by the painter to suit his or her painting needs. After all, there were many shade differences in the dyes used in clothing manufacturing, especially in the South.

The figure used in this book was sculpted by Mike Stelzel and is produced by his company, Michael-Roberts Ltd. It is typical of the high quality of today's commercially produced American Civil War miniatures. The figure is composed mainly of resin parts. While resin seems to be the trend, many companies use the traditional white metal alloy for their figures. I have worked with both and find very little difference in the two, except for a lighter weight with the resin castings.

I hope this book will help and inspire you to paint figures from this very interesting and important period of American history.

Military Miniature Clubs

Historical Miniature Society of Northeastern Oklahoma
5526 S. Toledo Place
Tulsa, OK 74135

Military Miniature Society of Illinois
P.O. Box 394
Skokie, IL 60077

Southern California Area Miniature Modeler's Society
31335 Arabasca Circle
Temecula, CA 92592

The Atlanta Soldier Society
2720 Towne Village Drive
Duluth, GA 30316

Colorado Miniature Figure Artists Association
15107 E. Hampden
Aurora, CO 80014

The Long Island Historical Miniature Collectors Society
P.O. Box 118
Wantagh, NY 11793

The Military Figure Collectors of New England
Lodge Road
Natick, MA 01760

Hudson Valley Historical Miniatures Guild Ltd.
P.O. Box 586
Pleasant Valley, NY 12569

Miniature Figure Collectors of America
19 Mars Road, North Star
Newark, DE 19711

The Fraternity of North American Military Miniature Artists
346 Derbyshire Lane
Riva, MD 21140

Virginia Company of Military Figure Collectors
11925 Smoke Tree Drive
Richmond, VA 23236

National Capital Model Soldier Society Inc.
14613 Stonehouse Court
Silver Spring, MD 20905

Milwaukee Military Miniature Modelers
2112 N. 67th Street
Wauwatosa, WI 53213

Preparations

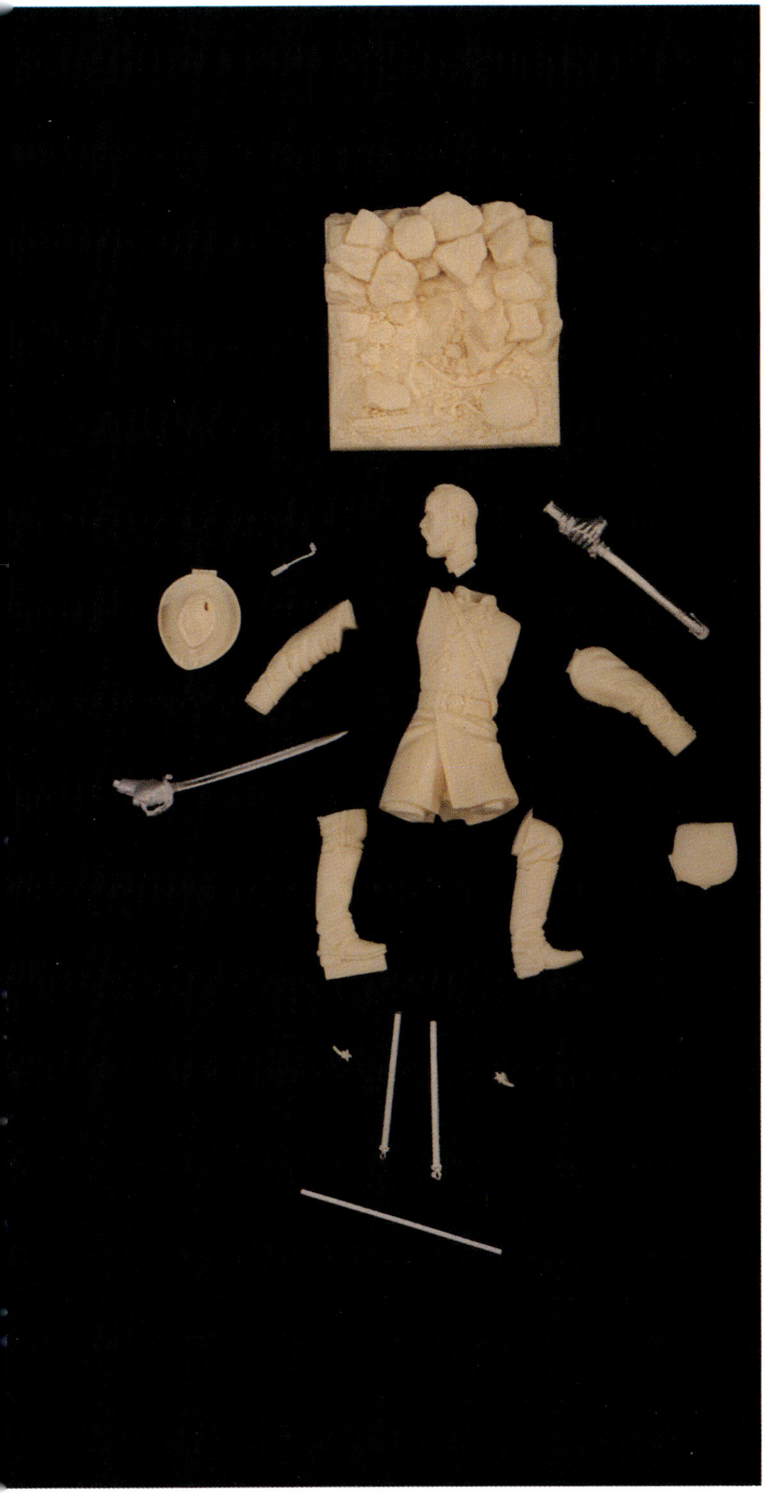

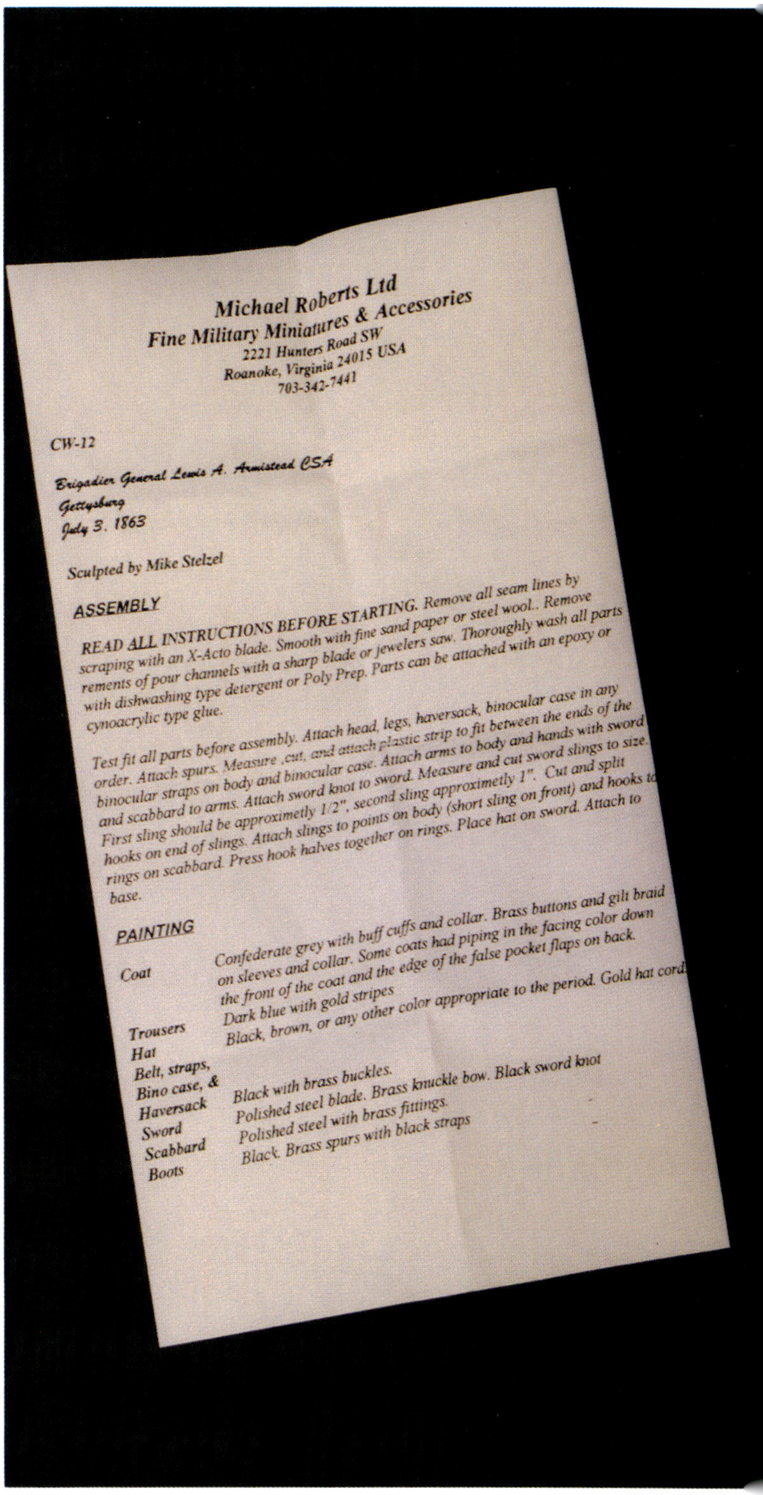

This kit is of Confederate Brigadier General Lewis A. Armistead at the Battle of Gettysburg. He is depicted charging the Union lines, surmounting their low rock wall during Pickett's Charge, moments before his death. These are the basic parts that you get when you buy the kit.

Carefully read the instructions.

The basic tools necessary for the clean up and construction of the kit.

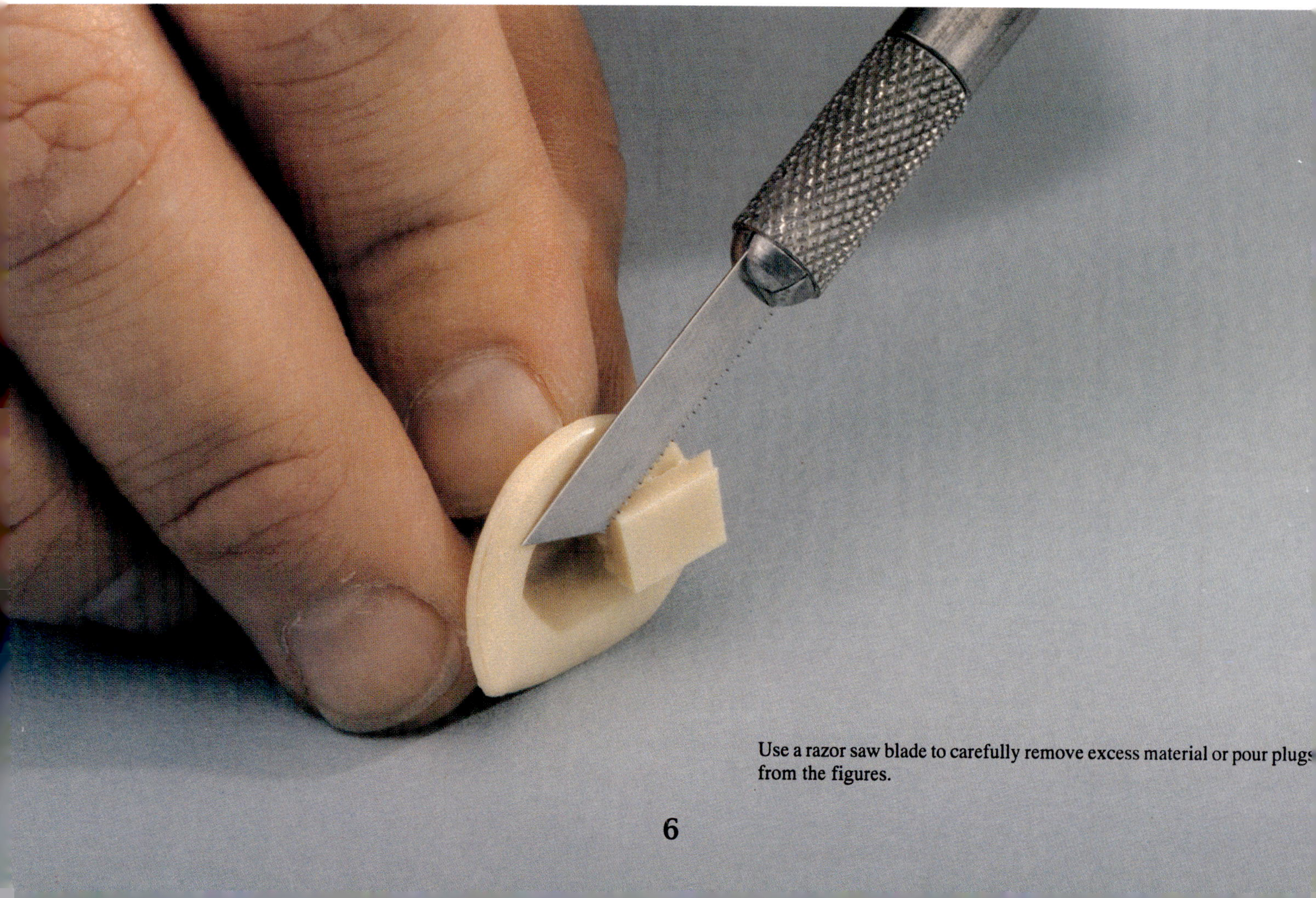

Use a razor saw blade to carefully remove excess material or pour plugs from the figures.

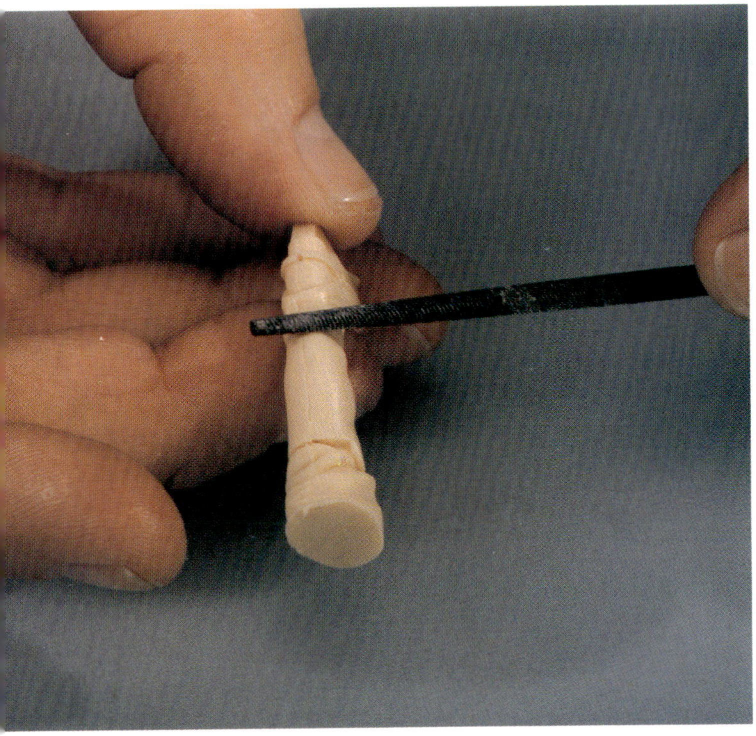

Using miniature files, reduce or file off any seam lines. Then smooth with fine sand paper or steel wool.

For larger areas, such as the base, you can smooth the piece using a large piece of sandpaper lying on a flat surface. Use a circular motion while sanding.

Two main types of glue are used, five minute epoxy and the quicker drying cyanoacrylate. The cyanoacrylate glues work very well with resin figures. The five minute epoxy is preferred when working on metal figures.

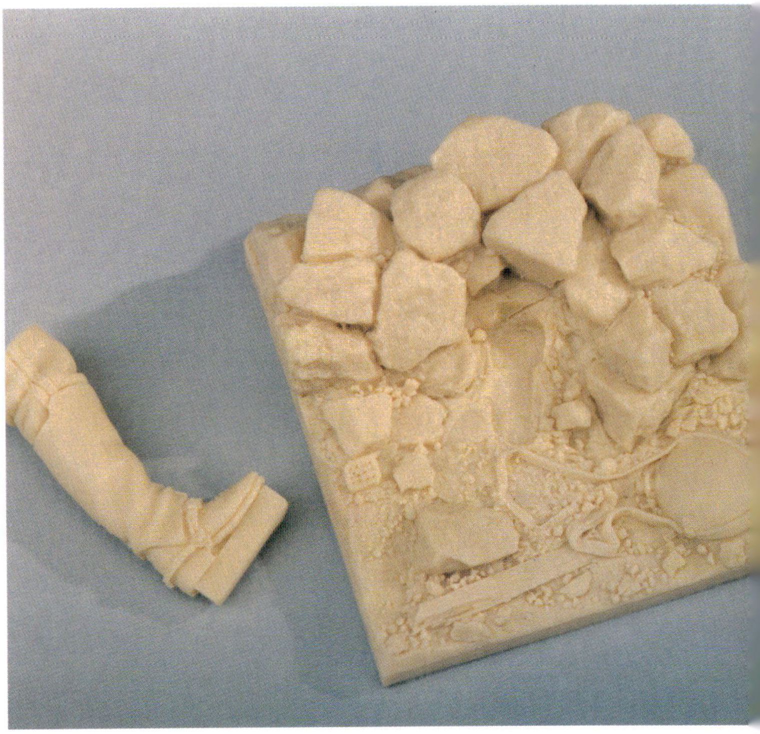

In the case of this figure, I chose to leave the peg on the bottom of the foot and drill out an appropriate area in the base. This way I can insert the peg into the slot and more securely hold the finished figure to the base.

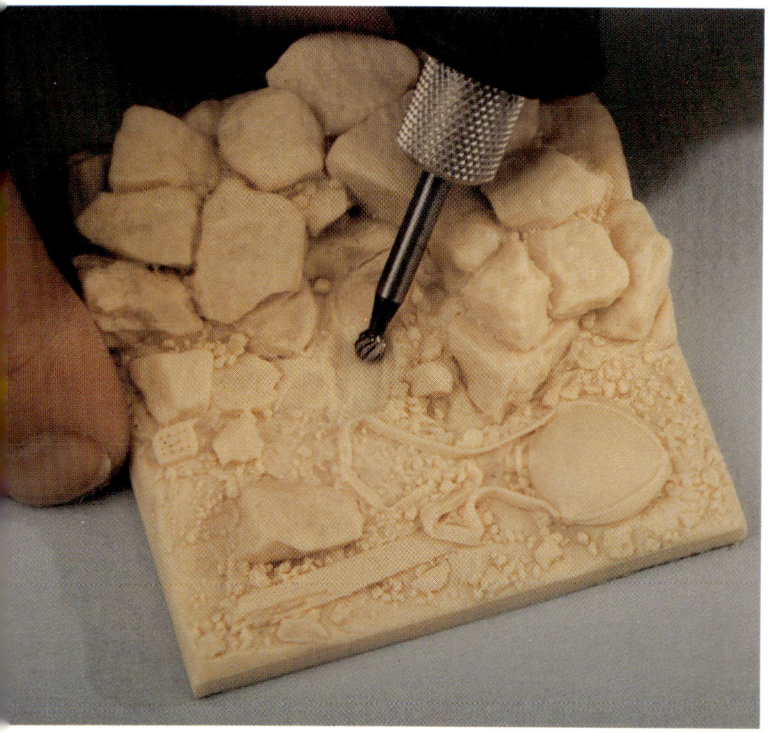

Using a burr, I form a slotted area in the display base to receive the peg on the base of the foot.

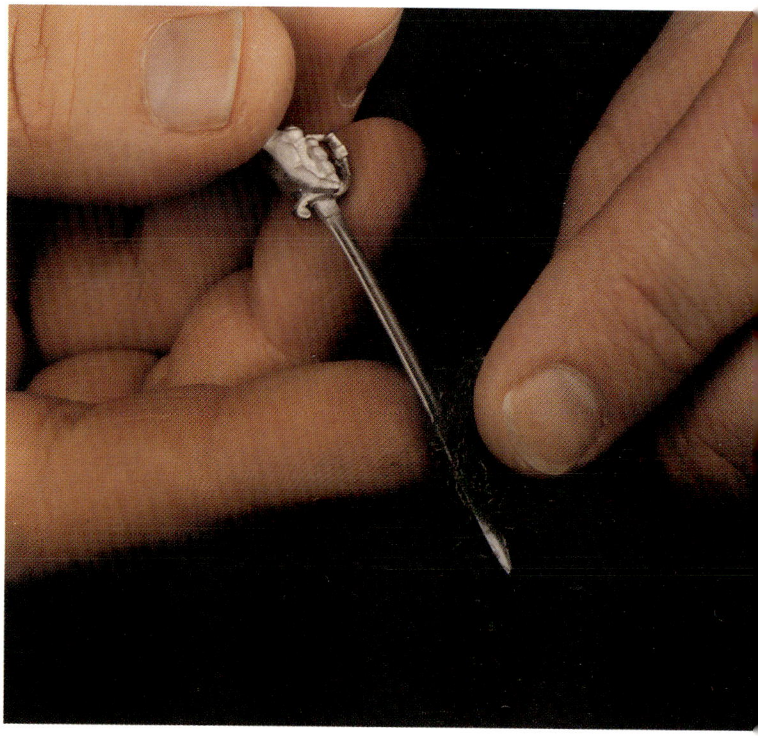

Then you can polish the white metal surfaces with very fine steel wool.

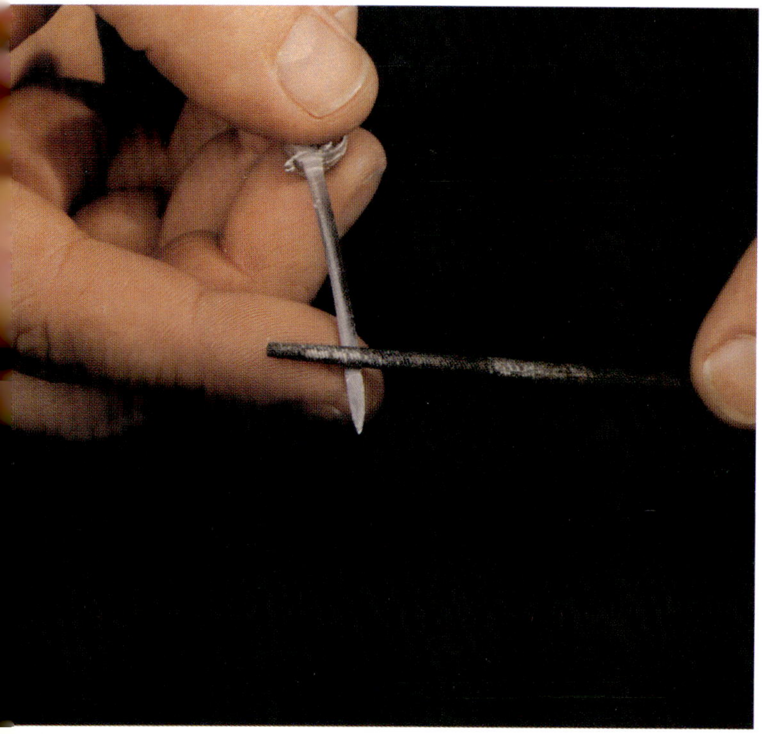

The next phase of the clean-up deals with metal parts. Real swords and scabbards were both made of steel. The miniature versions have been reproduced in white metal. As such, instead of painting them silver, you can burnish them or buff them out and let the actual metal represent natural metal.
First smooth down any rough edges with a very fine toothed file.

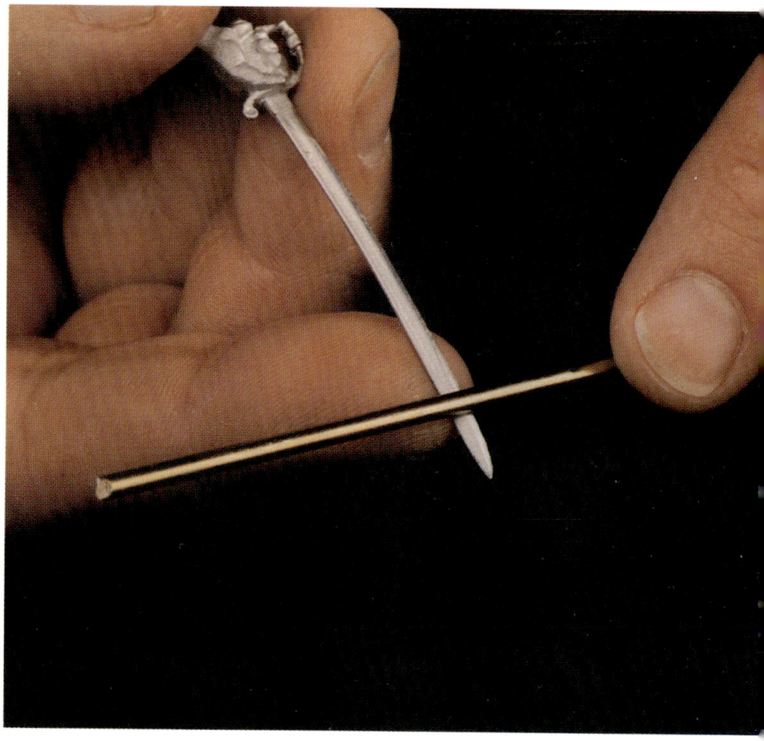

Next burnish the white metal parts using any type of metal tool you prefer. This could be a dental pick, a brass rod or any other item that is harder than the metal you are polishing. We will cover final detailing later in the book.

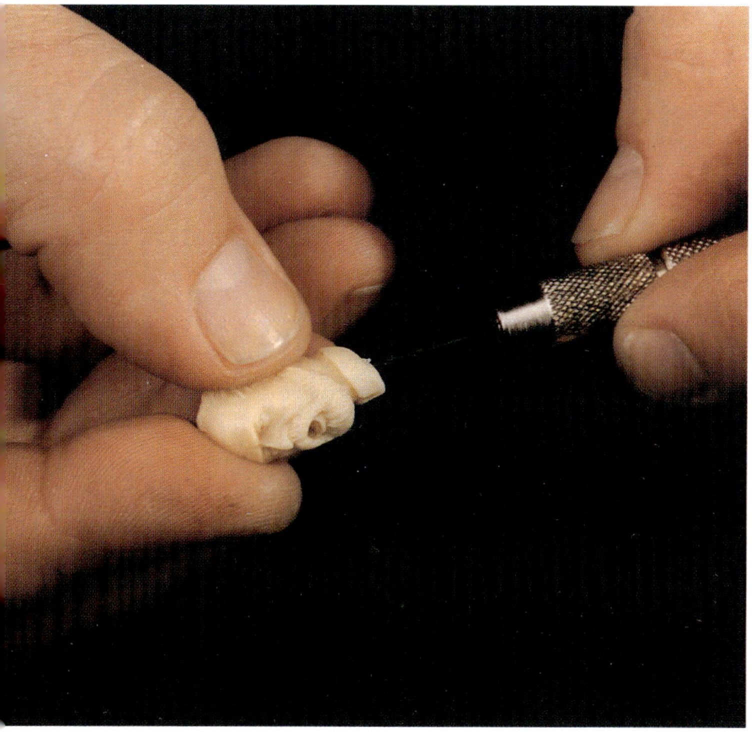

Moving on to the head, drill a small hole in the bottom of the neck and insert a paper clip or a toothpick. This will make the painting task easier than if the head were attached to the body.

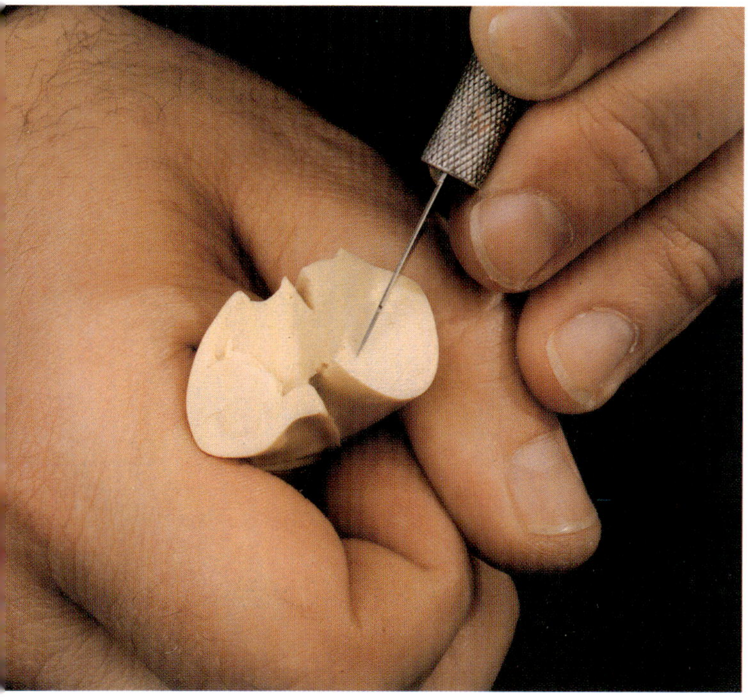

Cross hatch the surfaces that will be glued together. If you prefer, you can drill small holes into each surface to be joined to achieve the same effect. This gives the glue more holding power.

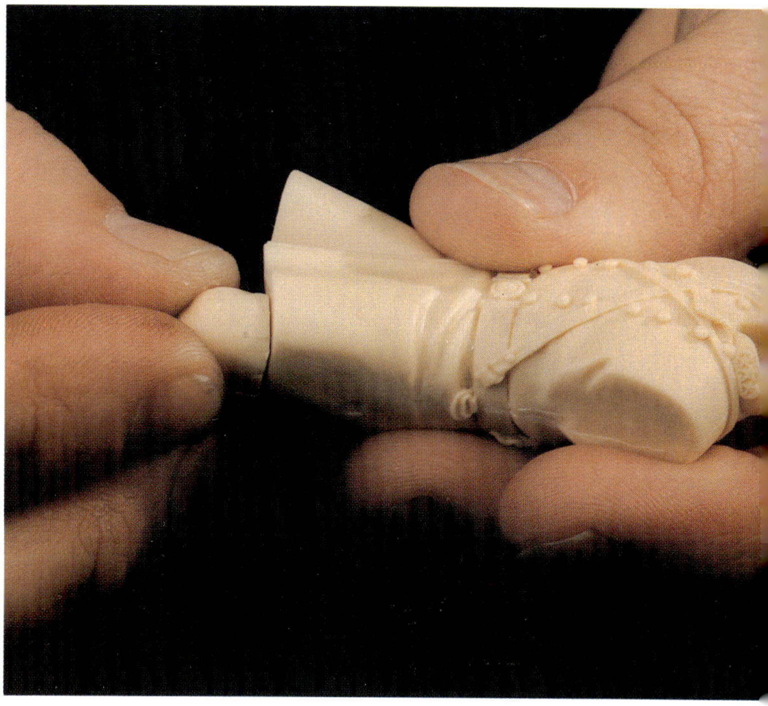

I prefer to assemble as much of the figure as possible before I prime and start my painting. Before gluing, test fit each piece to insure proper fit.

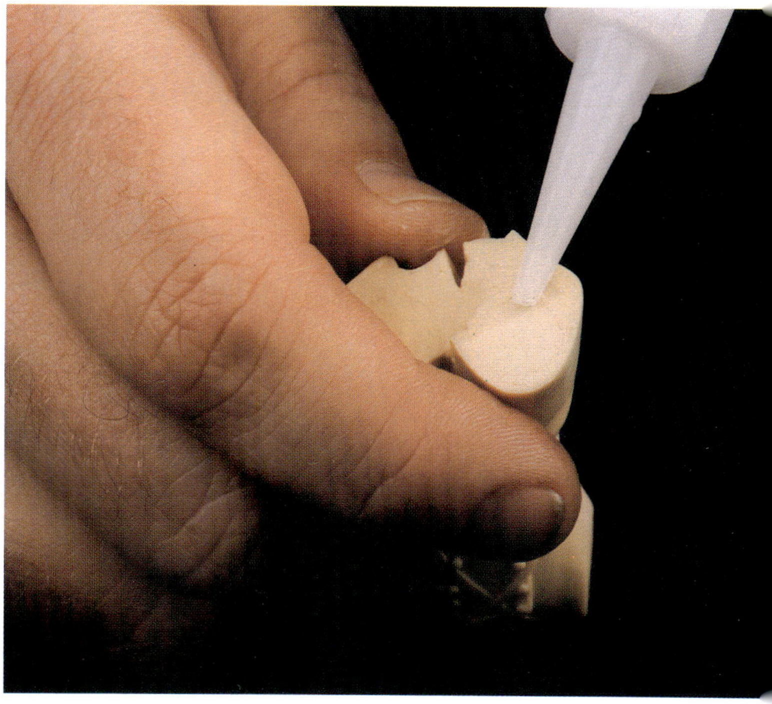

Glue the pieces together with cyanoacrylate.

Of great importance to this figure is the proper alignment of the legs. With the legs improperly aligned, the general will either not clear the wall or will appear to be dancing on it.

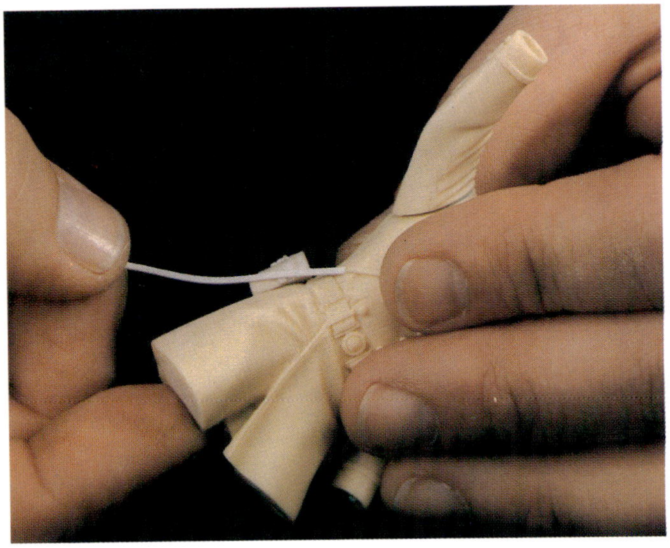

To extend the binocular strap away from the body and onto the case, I added the remainder of the strap provided in the kit. First glue one end of the strap material to the strap that was sculpted onto the figure.

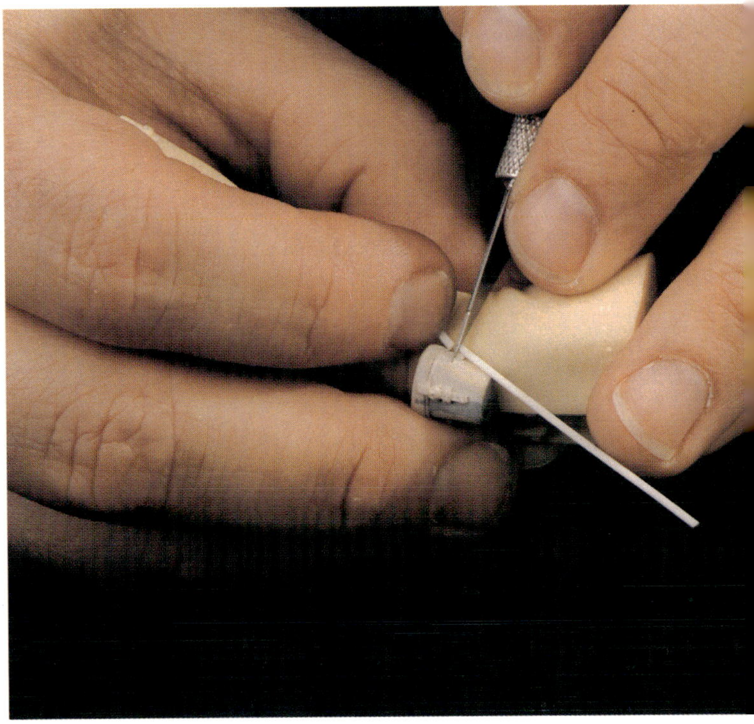

Before gluing the other end to the binocular case, I cut off the excess strapping material.

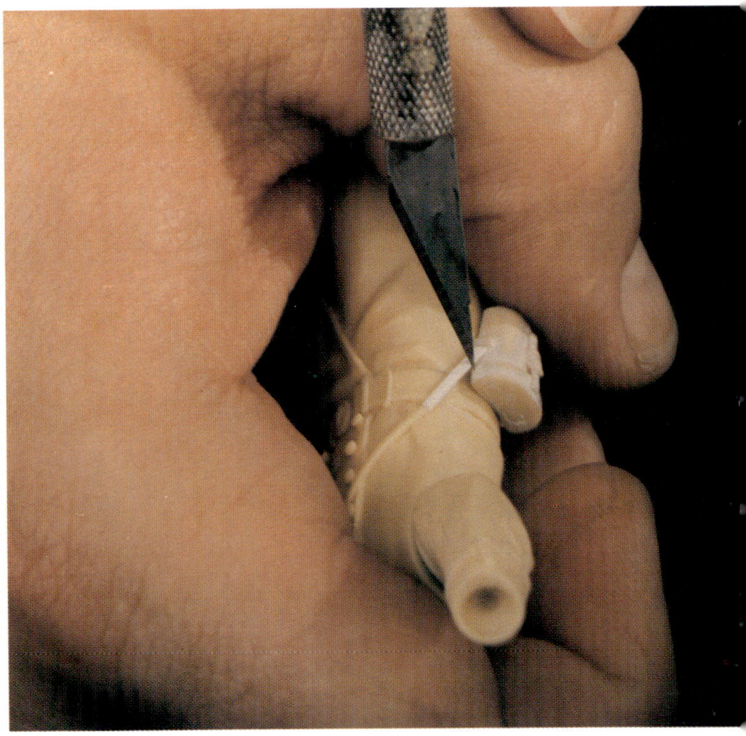

What I do next is apply a small drop of glue to the attachment point on the binocular case.
In the case of figures with burnished metal parts, including this figure, we will wait until after we have primed the body to affix them and any straps attached to them. We will return to these pieces later.

Painting the Figure

Next I primed the figure and its base, allowing them to dry thoroughly.

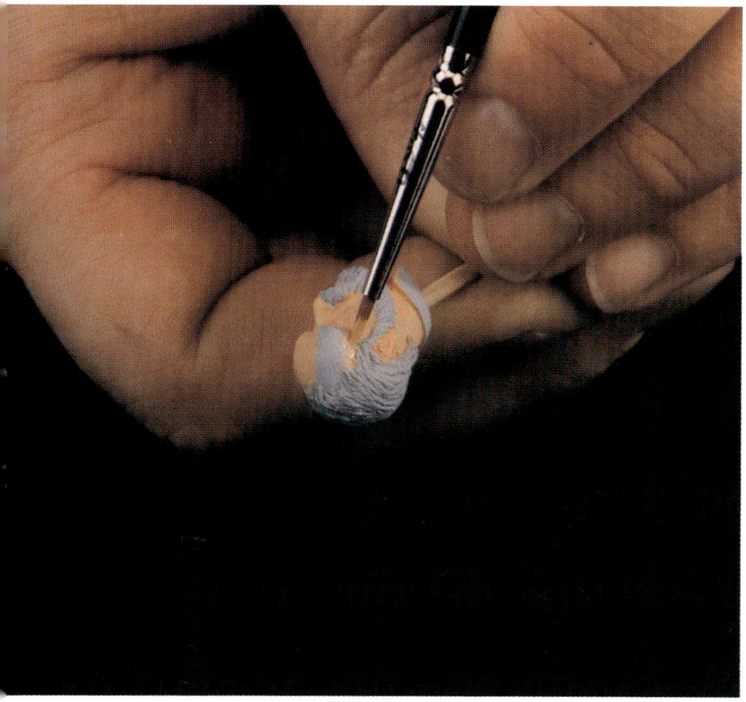

At this point I undercoat the entire figure in the appropriate colors of hobby paints, blue for the pants, gray for the jacket, etc.

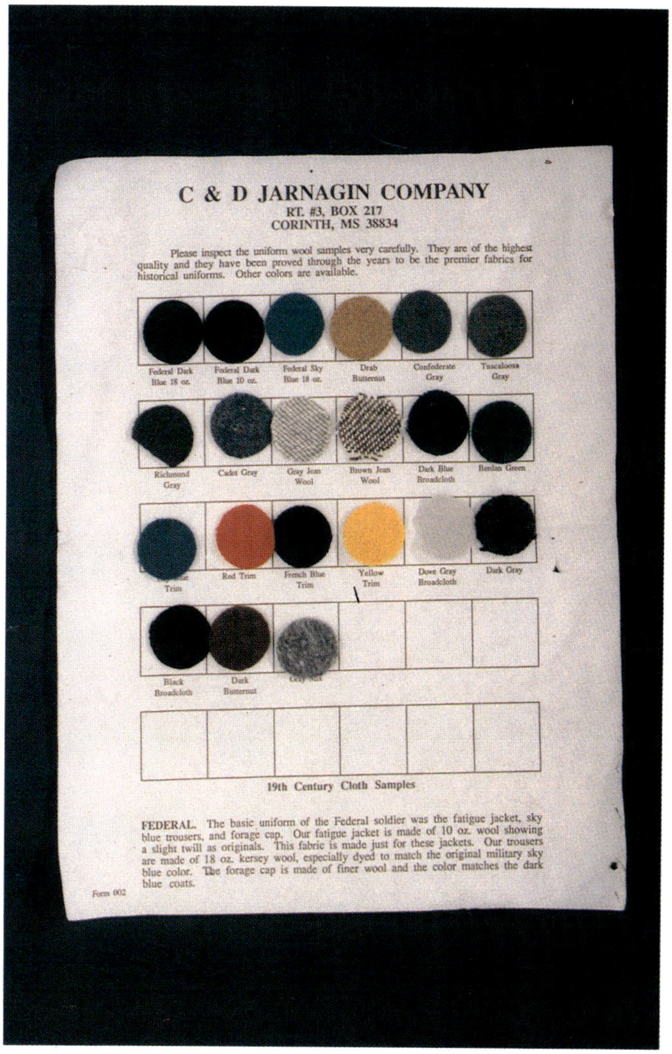

To ensure accuracy, reference materials are important when painting figures. Such materials include books and photographs - or in the case of Civil War figures, color illustrations, and fabric samples from companies which supply authentic uniforms to re-enacting groups.

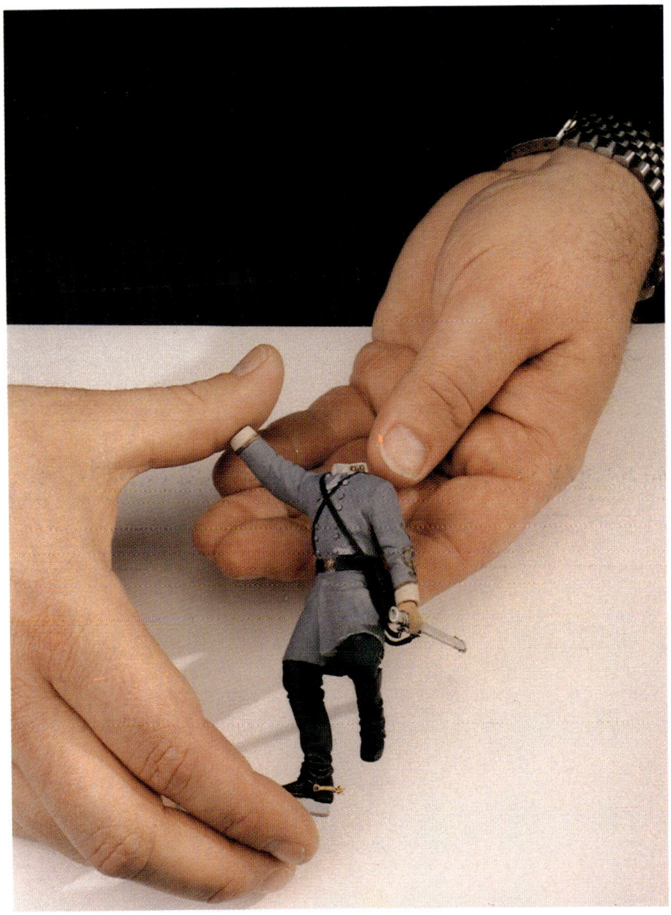

The undercoated figure with all appropriate colors applied to the correct areas. The burnished sword and scabbard with straps are now in place and undercoated as needed.

Don't forget to undercoat the base as well.

The undercoating of the base is finished. For the rocks I used a dark gray which will become my shadow color. Let that thoroughly dry. We arc now rcady to bcgin thc highlighting. It is not ncccssary on this base to have undercoated every little item, i.e. the piece of hardtack and the straps of the canteen. When we finish the dirt, we will have to come back and paint them as they are sure to get some of the dirt colored paint on them.

I add white to the dark gray that I used on the rocks to achieve my first highlight color.

Load your brush with this color and wipe off the excess until there is very little paint coming off of the brush.

By lightly dragging the brush over the entire surface of the rocks you start picking out just the raised highlights. This light gray is used on the rocks only. The same highlighting technique will be used over the entire surface of the base.

Using the lightest highlight color (created by adding more white to the first highlight color), selectively pick out just the highest area of the rocks.

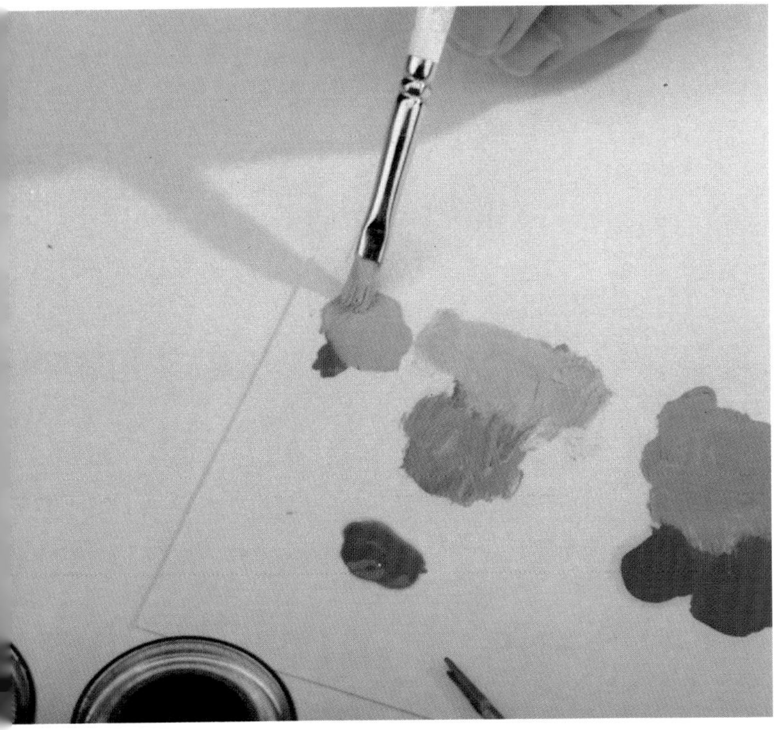

Mix in some of the ground color with the lightest gray and go back over some of your light highlights. This ties the rocks in with the dirt to give them a dusty appearance. Use a light touch to keep this very subtle.

The same techniques are used when painting the ground as were used on the rocks. Here we are applying the highlight color to the ground.

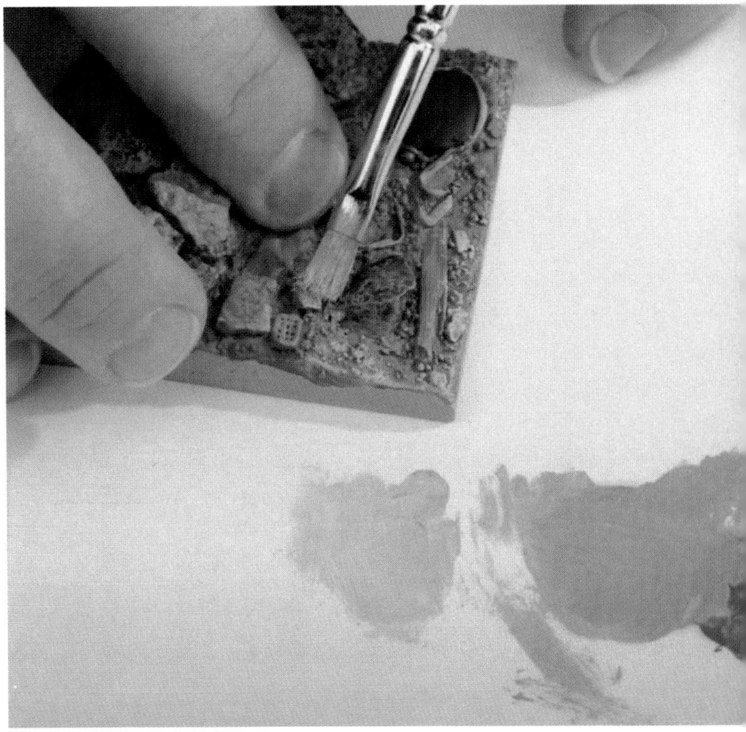

The light highlight being added.

Mix in a little of the ground color with the light highlight of the rocks to tie in the rock color with the ground while picking up the details of the small pebbles. The hardtack, the broken wood and any other battlefield debris will be painted using the same technique, painting the dark first, then the highlight followed by the light highlight.

Using the dry brush technique, I then apply a lighter shade of brown as my first highlight.

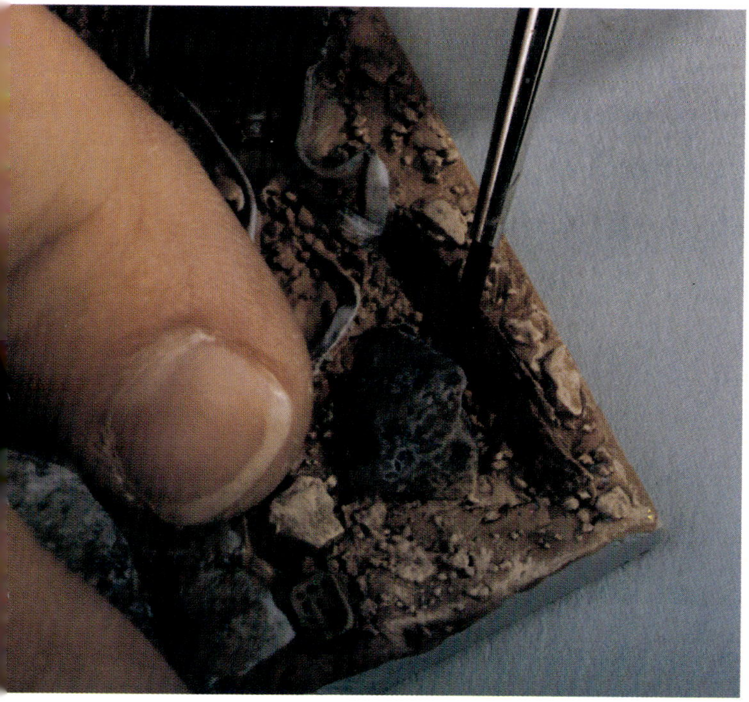

For the wood debris on the base, I first paint it dark brown. Let this dry completely.

I then mix white to this brown to create a light highlight color.

The light highlight color is carefully applied, making sure that the edges of the wood and any other raised areas are covered.

The wood is finished.

Hard tack was like a large soda cracker. These are the colors I will use to paint the hard tack. They are Burnt Sienna, Yellow Ocher, and White.

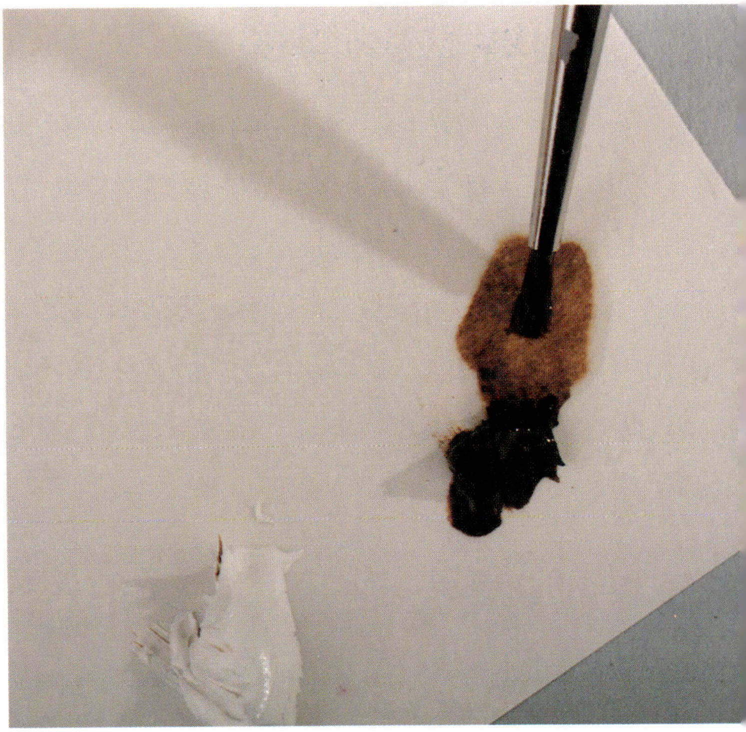

First thin down some Burnt Sienna to make a wash.

Apply the wash to the top of the hard tack. This will run into the recessed areas and will accent the holes in the hard tack.

Next mix White and a small amount of Yellow Ocher to create a slightly yellowish off-white color.

Dry brush this color across the top and sides of the hard tack.

Progress.

Highlight the edges with white.

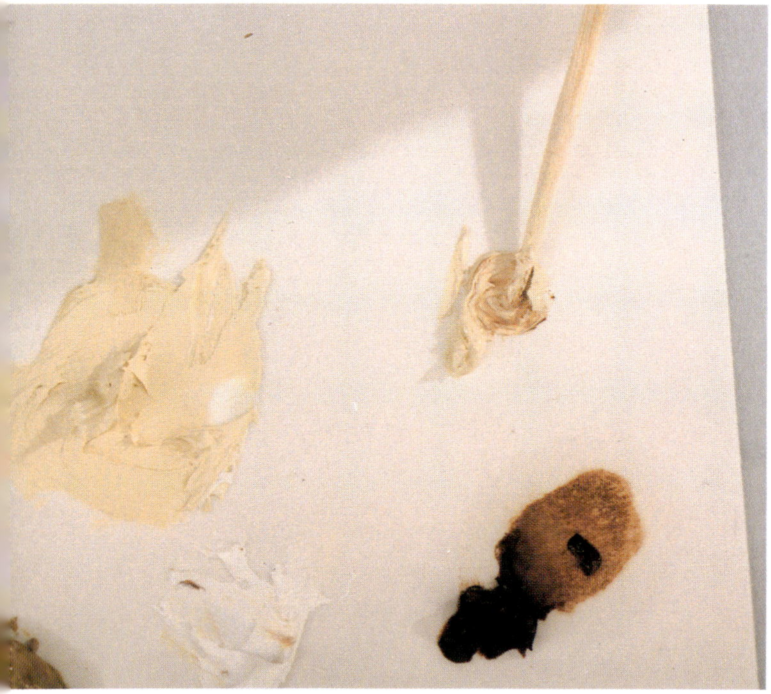

Add a small amount of Burnt Sienna into your White and Yellow Ocher mix to create a toasted surface. We will apply this color randomly to the

top of the hard tack, achieving the look of a modern soda cracker. Apply this color using a dry brush in a dabbing motion.

Paint the undercoated canteen cover with raw umber along strap lines and in other locations where shadows are needed.

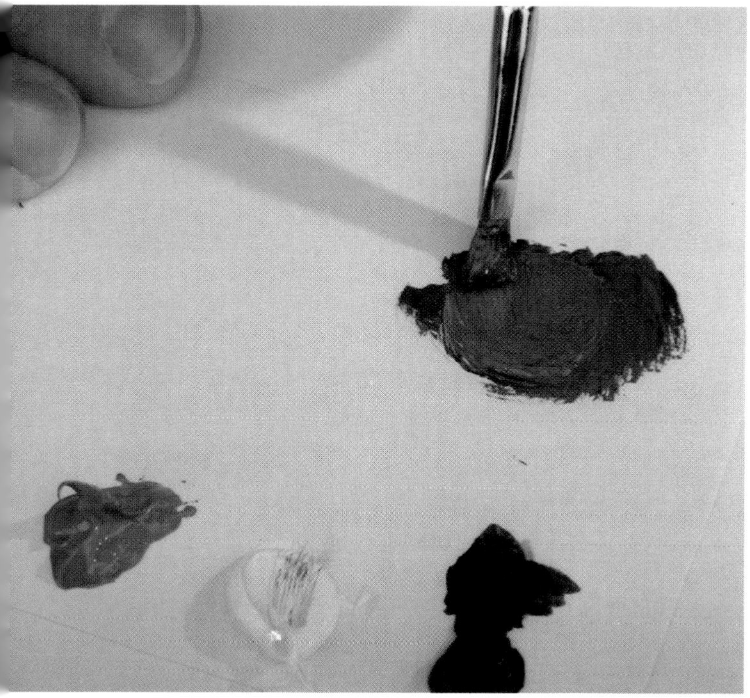

The middle color is made by adding raw umber, white, and a small amount of yellow ocher.

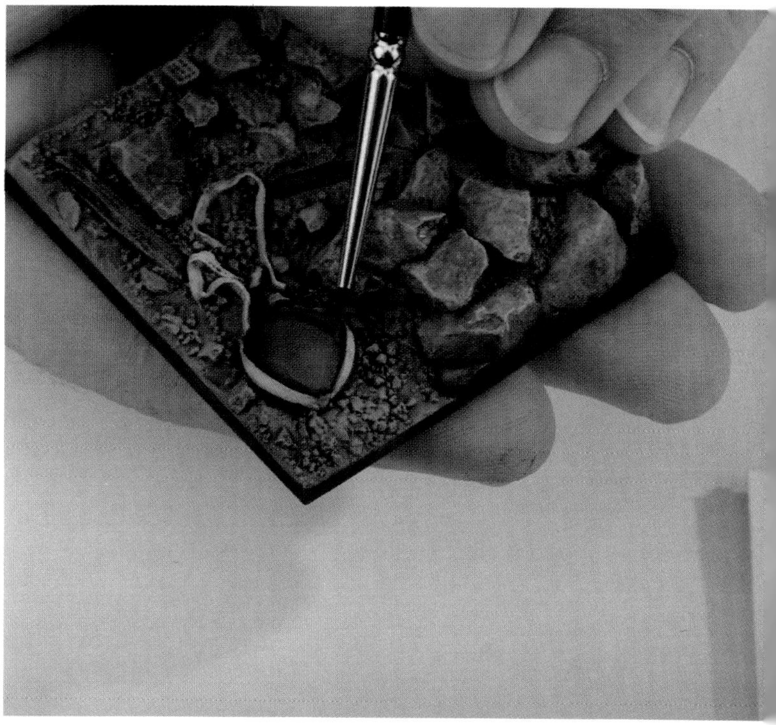

Blending the middle and shadow colors.

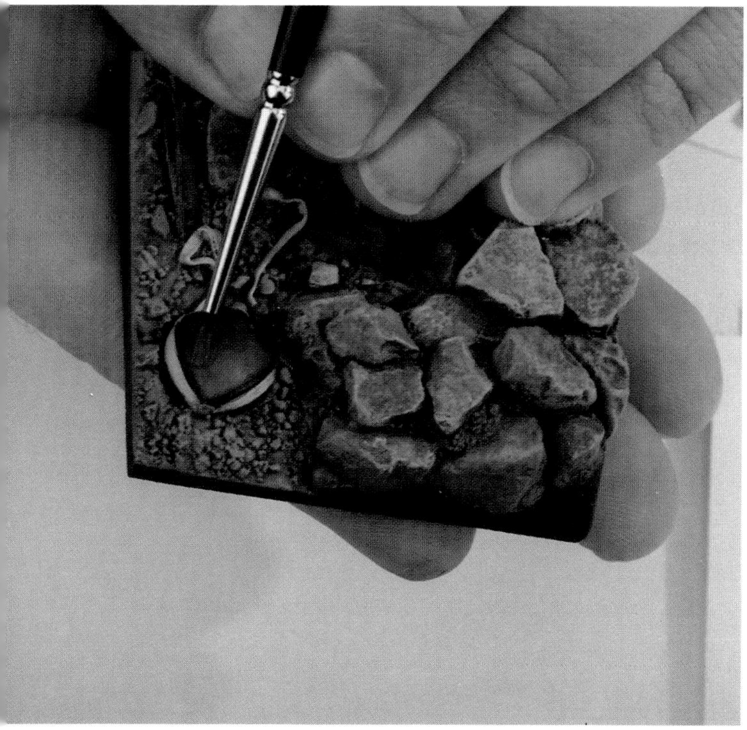

Bring this middle color up to the shadow lines and then blend the two where they meet, creating the desired effect of a soft transition between the two.

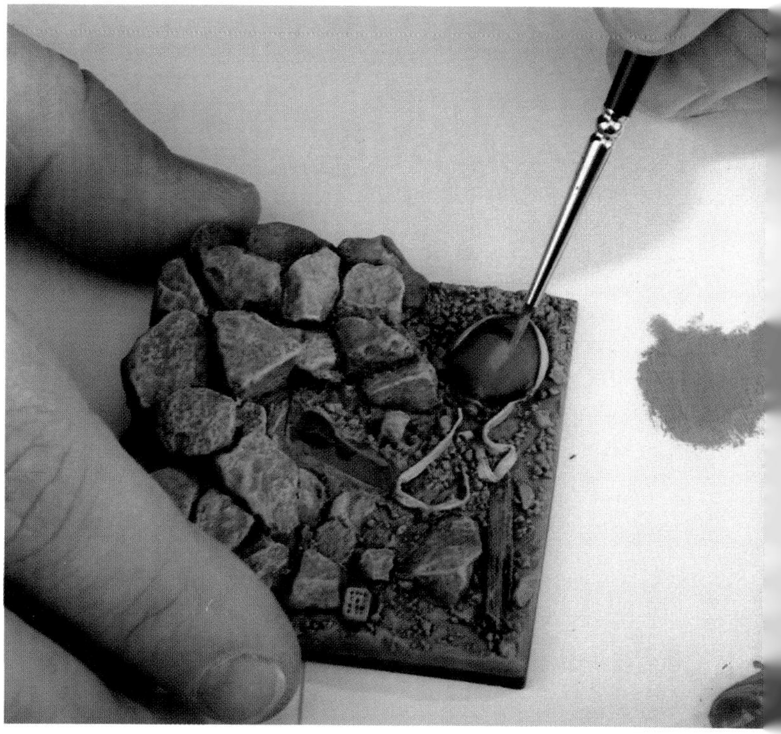

Adding a little more yellow ocher and some white to the middle color provides the light highlights, which are four or five shades above the middle color. Apply this color.

Blend in the light highlight as well.

Using our three shade technique of shadow, middle color and highlight, I've mixed browns and medium browns with white to create the shadow and middle colors of the strap on the canteen. Pure white is used for the highlights. This strap can be left very dark and dirty as it is lying on the battlefield. Here is the finished strap.

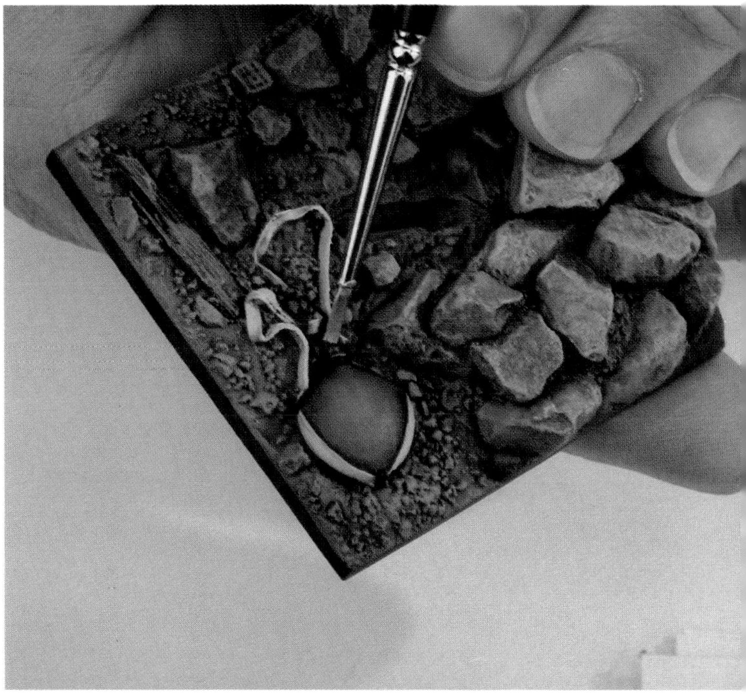

Painting metal items, I undercoat silver objects in black and gold objects in brown. This canteen body is made of tin. Its protruding neck and strap clips get the black undercoat. Then dry brush them with a dull silver.

I'm painting the leading edges of the base a deep brown so that this base will blend in well with the wooden pedestal I am going to attach it to.

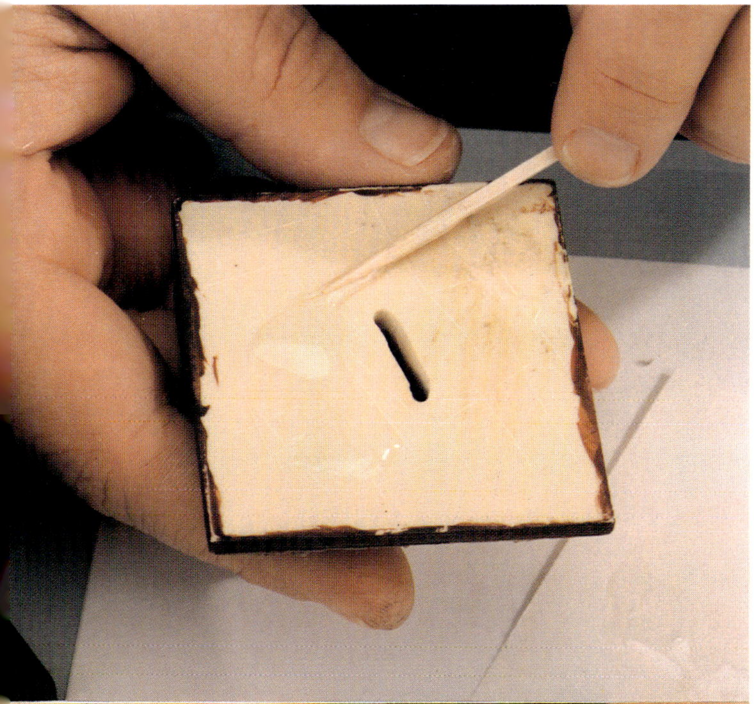

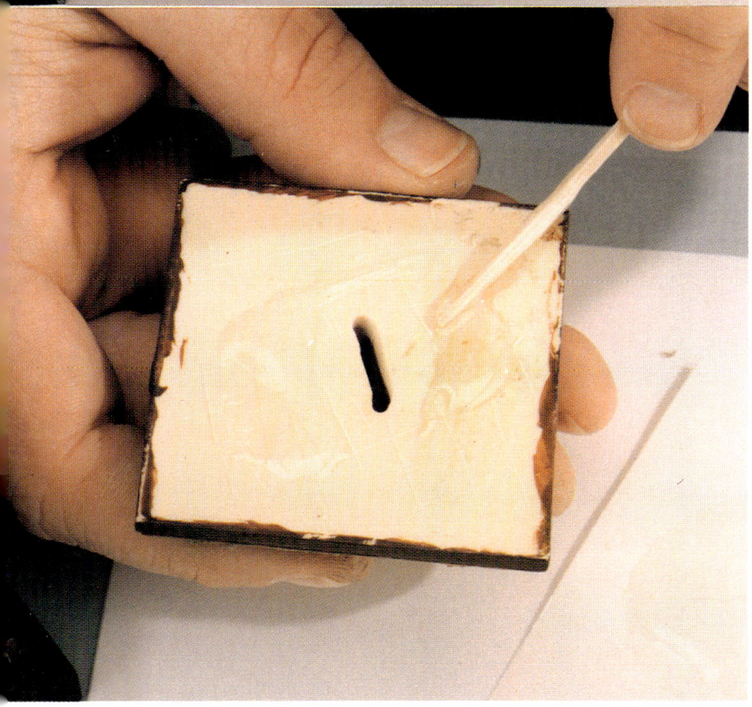

I will use five minute epoxy to attach the base to the wooden pedestal. Cross hatch both the base and pedestal to insure a strong bond.

Attach the undercoated figure to the base with five minute epoxy, checking for proper fit and position. The head and the hand with the sword will be added later.

The colors I use for Caucasian flesh are Titanium White, Yellow Ocher, Cadmium Red, Cadmium Yellow, and Burnt Sienna or Mars Brown.

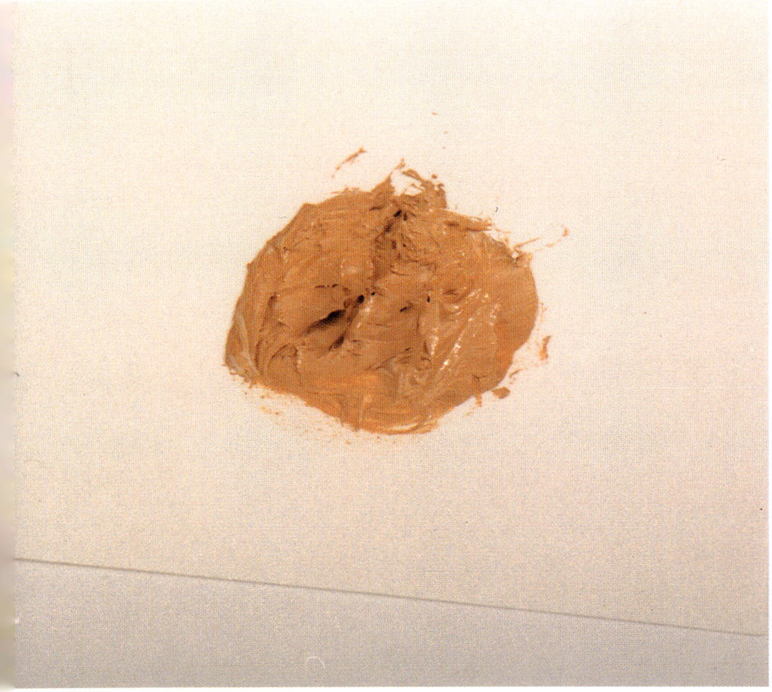

This is our basic flesh color, from which we will lighten and darken the face. While this is not an exact science as to proportions, the mixing of the five colors makes this basic Caucasian flesh tone.

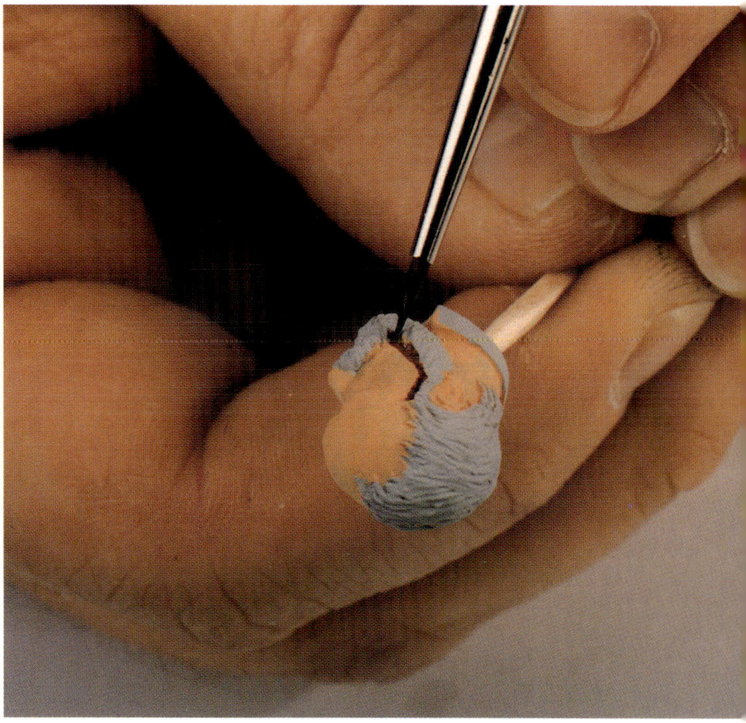

Burnt Sienna is applied where the beard, hair, and collar meet the skin.

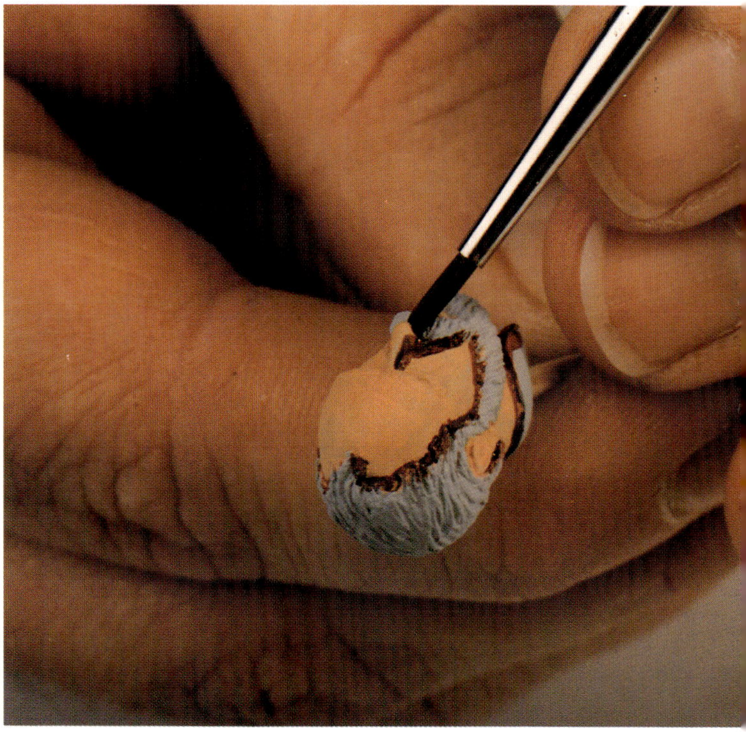

I also place this dark shadow color on the sides of the nose, the nostrils, the smile line ...

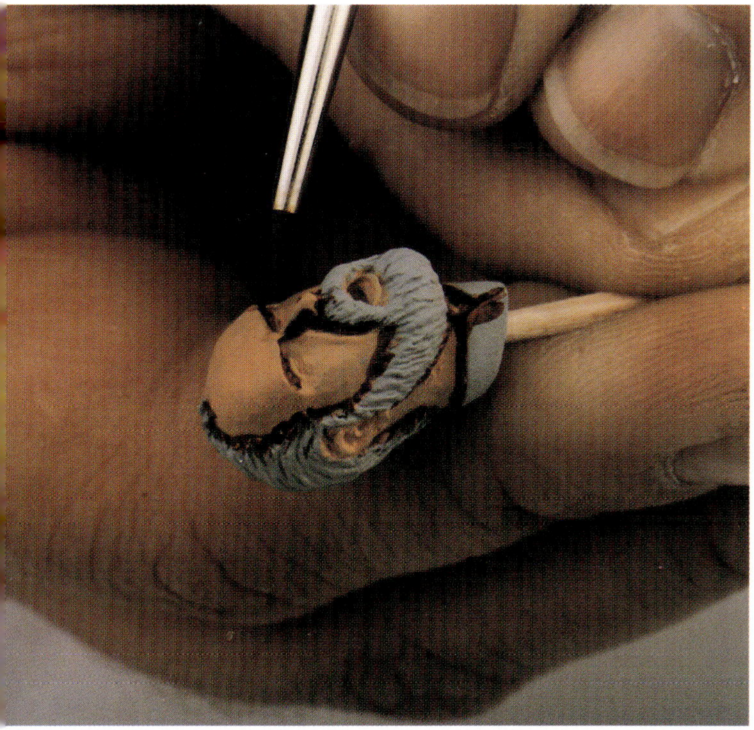

... under the brow ridges ...

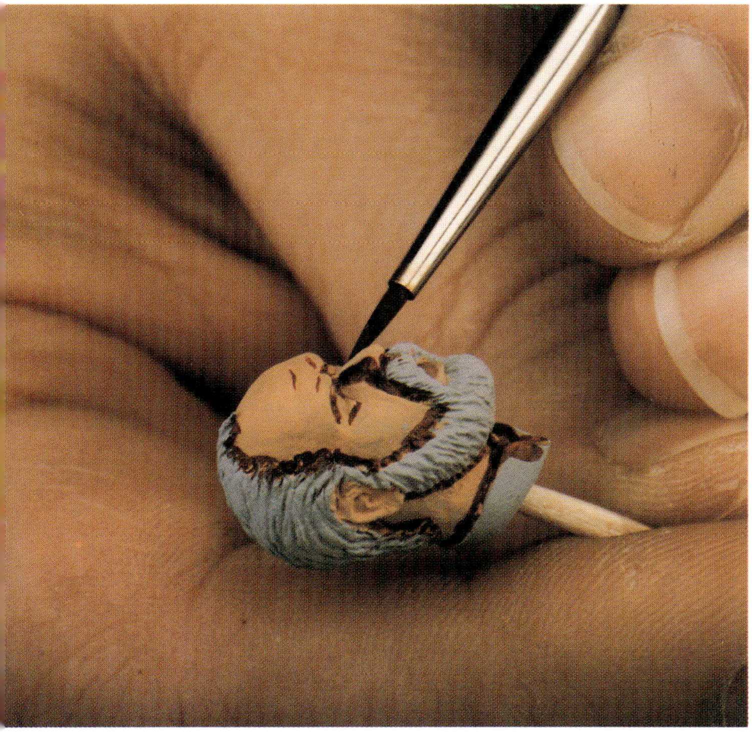

... in the frown lines and under the eyes.

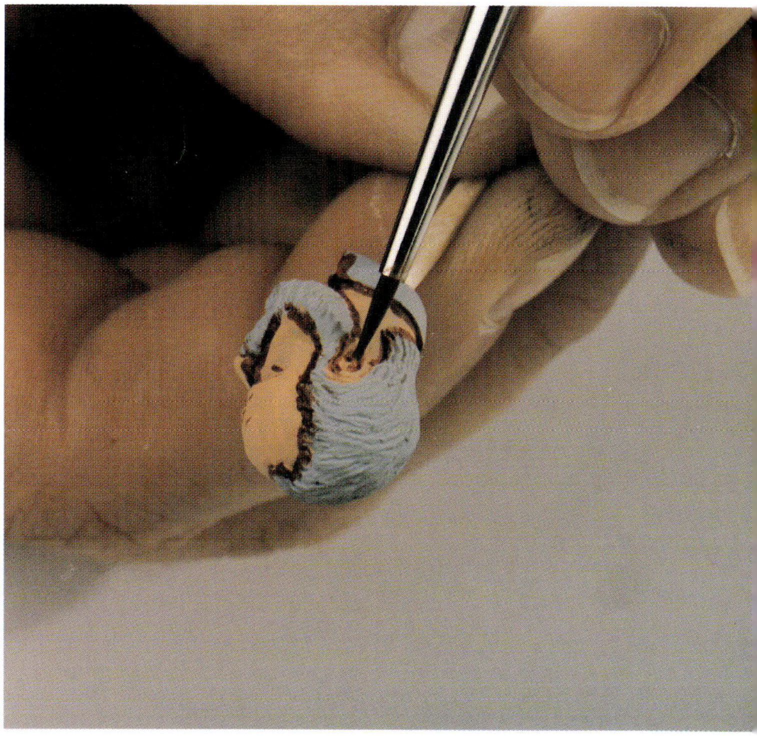

Also use the Burnt Sienna to shadow the insides of the ears.

And finally, shadow inside the mouth and under the lower lip.

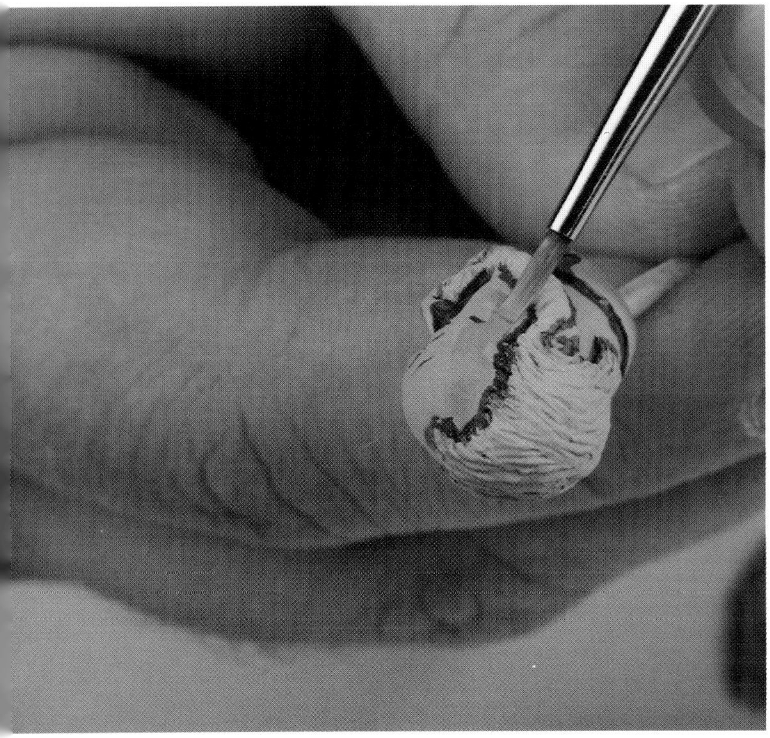

Apply the middle flesh tone to the face, bringing it right up to the shadow lines.

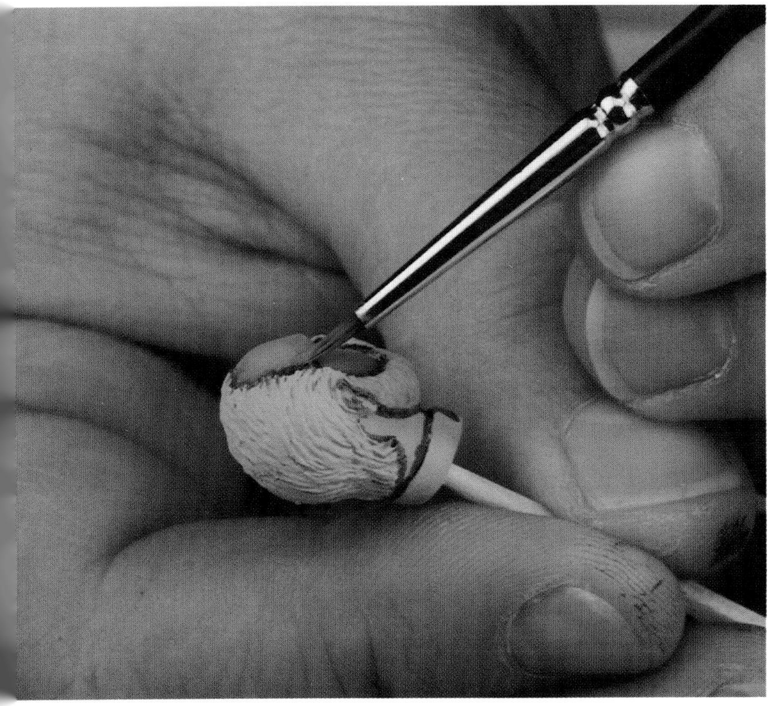

Now blend the shadows and the medium flesh tone to soften the lines of demarcation.

The blended lines.

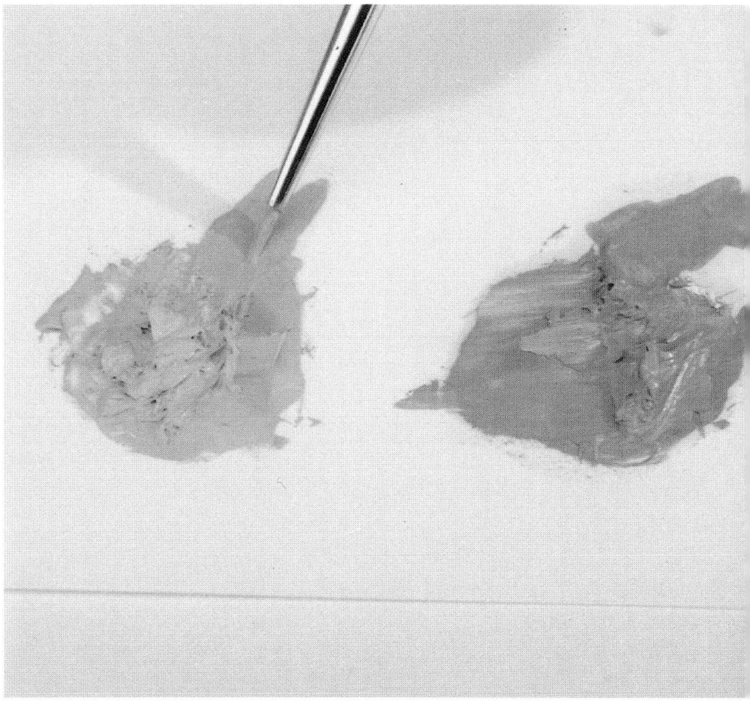

The highlight for the basic flesh color is created by adding white and a small amount of yellow to the basic flesh mix.

Apply the highlight color to the raised ridge of the smile line, the tip of the nose, the top of the ears, the top of the forehead, just below the eye on the lower lid, along the crest of the brow ridge, and along the top of the cheek bones.

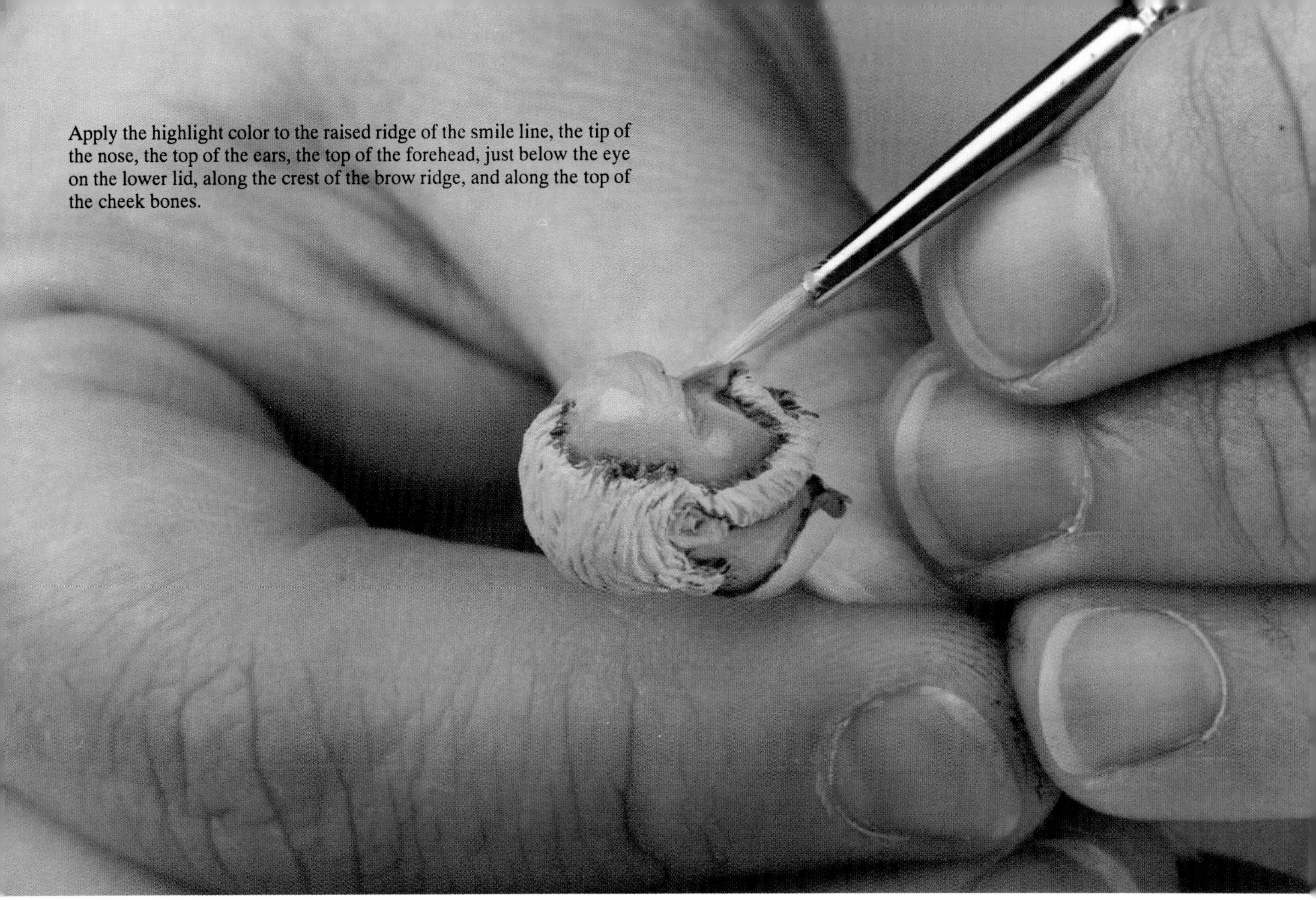

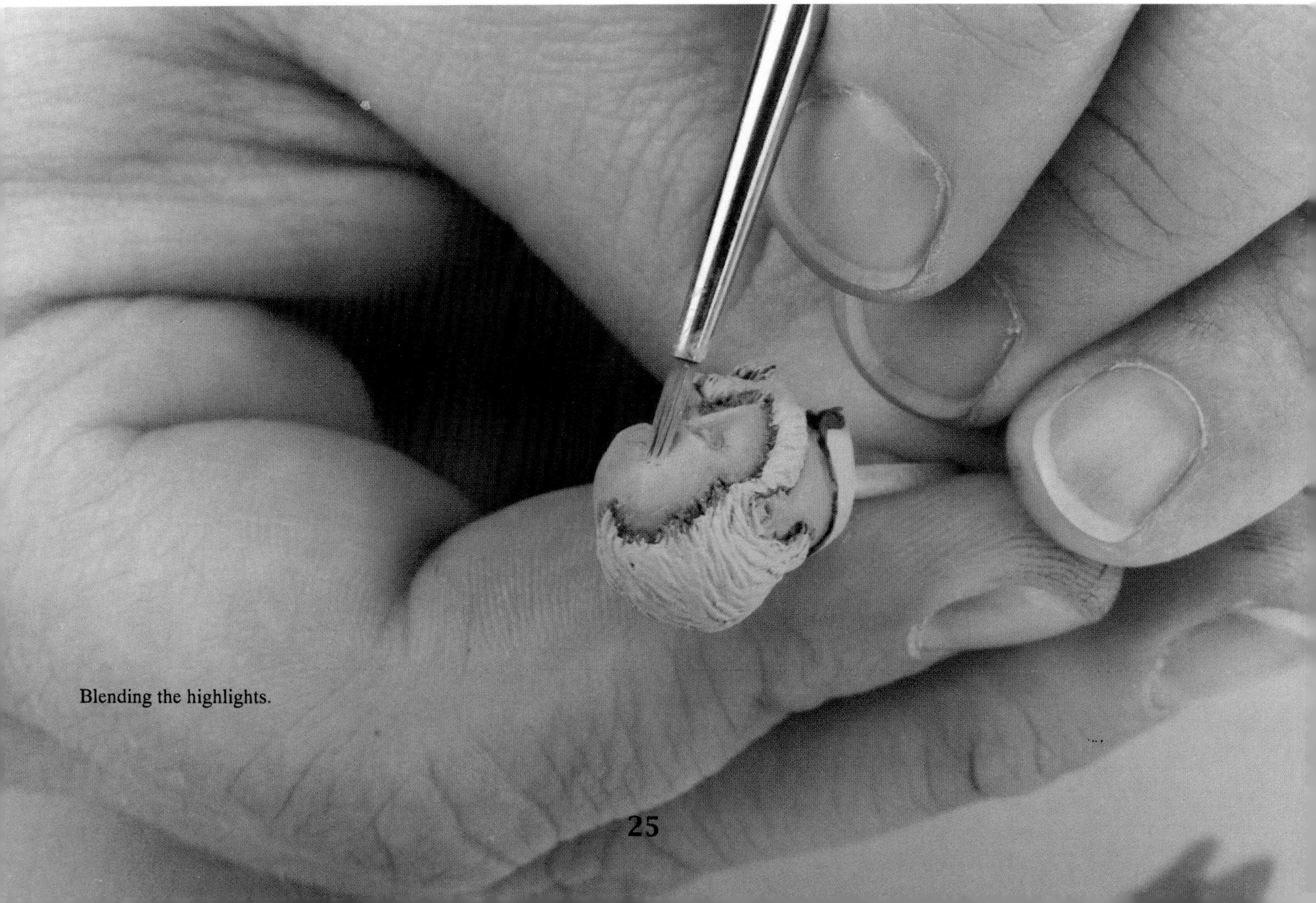

Blending the highlights.

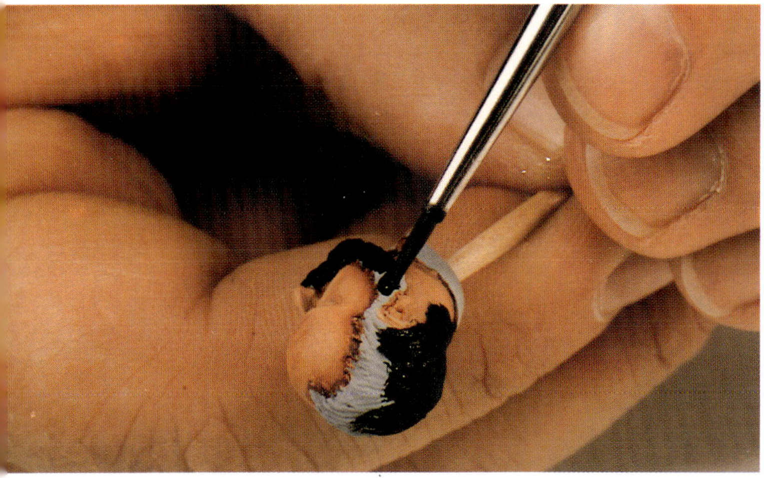

I undercoat the hair and beard in black hobby paint and allow it to dry completely before proceeding.

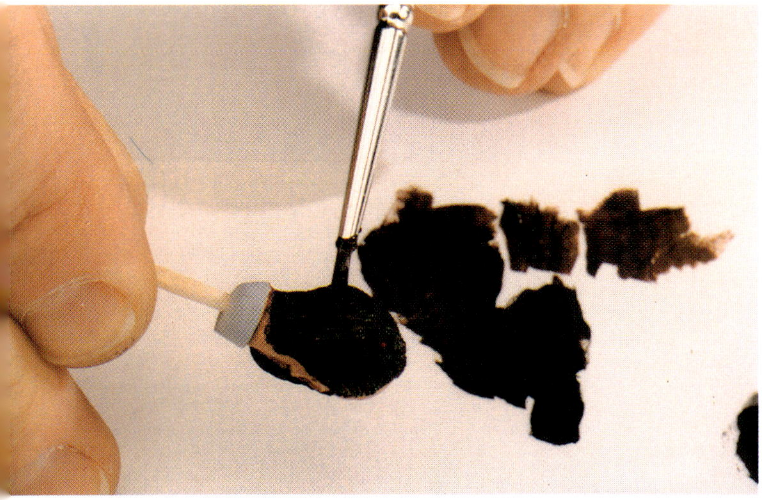

Using a dark brown and the same application method as used on the rocks of the base, I dry brushed a brown highlight all over the hair and beard.

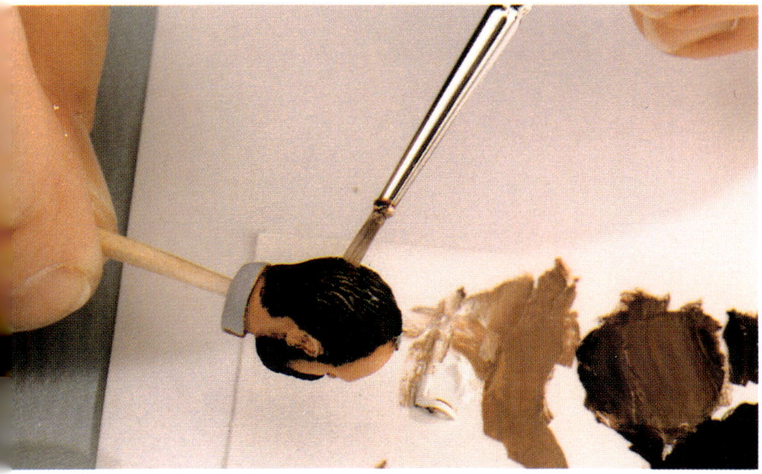

The light highlight is applied to specific areas (such as the top of the head, the front of the mustache and certain portions of the beard) to pull out light highlights.

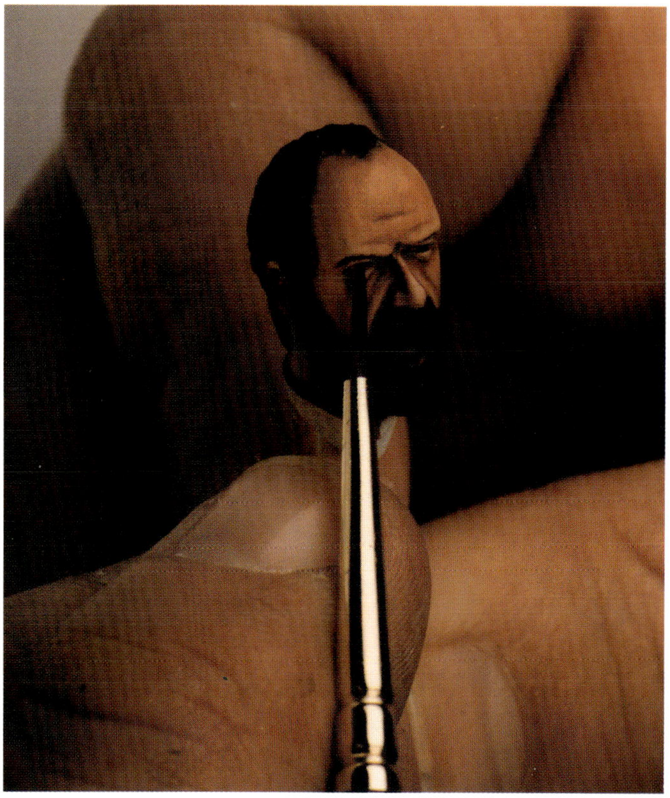

For the eyes, I place a black dot in the center of each eye. Armistead is squinting, and not much of the whites of his eyes would be visible. What little white would be visible will be put in next.

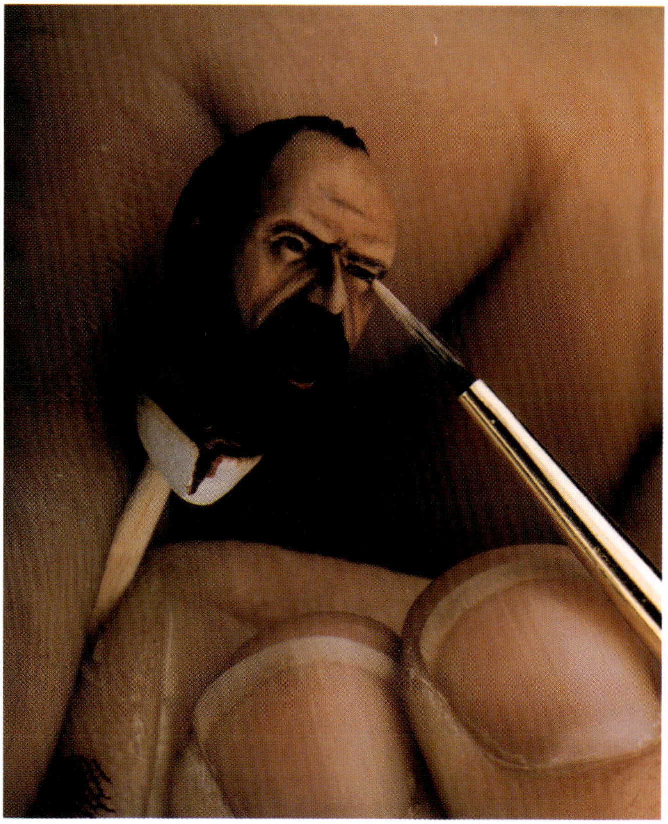

I mixed white with a little of the highlight flesh tone to create an off-white color for the whites of the eyes. Apply carefully.

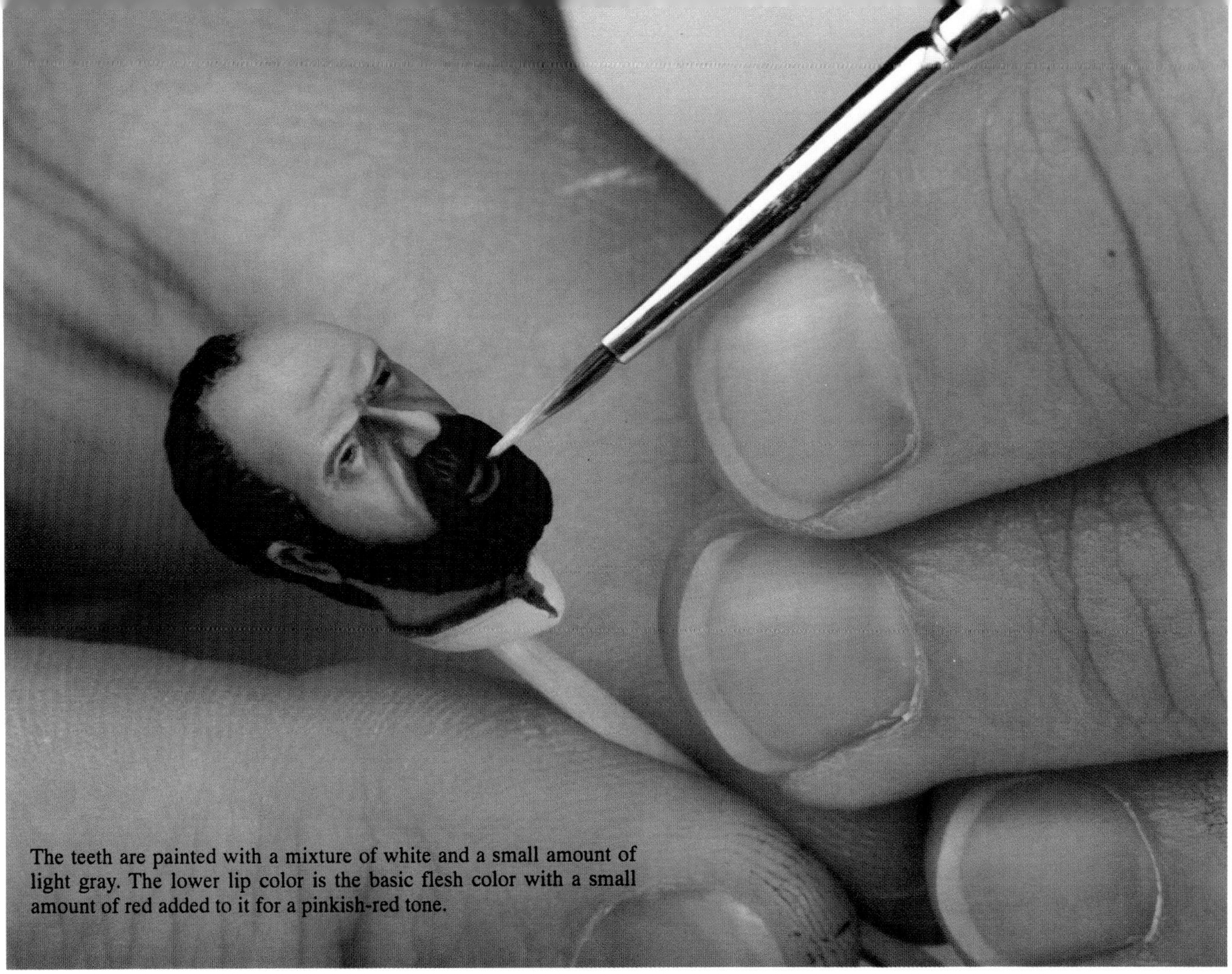

The teeth are painted with a mixture of white and a small amount of light gray. The lower lip color is the basic flesh color with a small amount of red added to it for a pinkish-red tone.

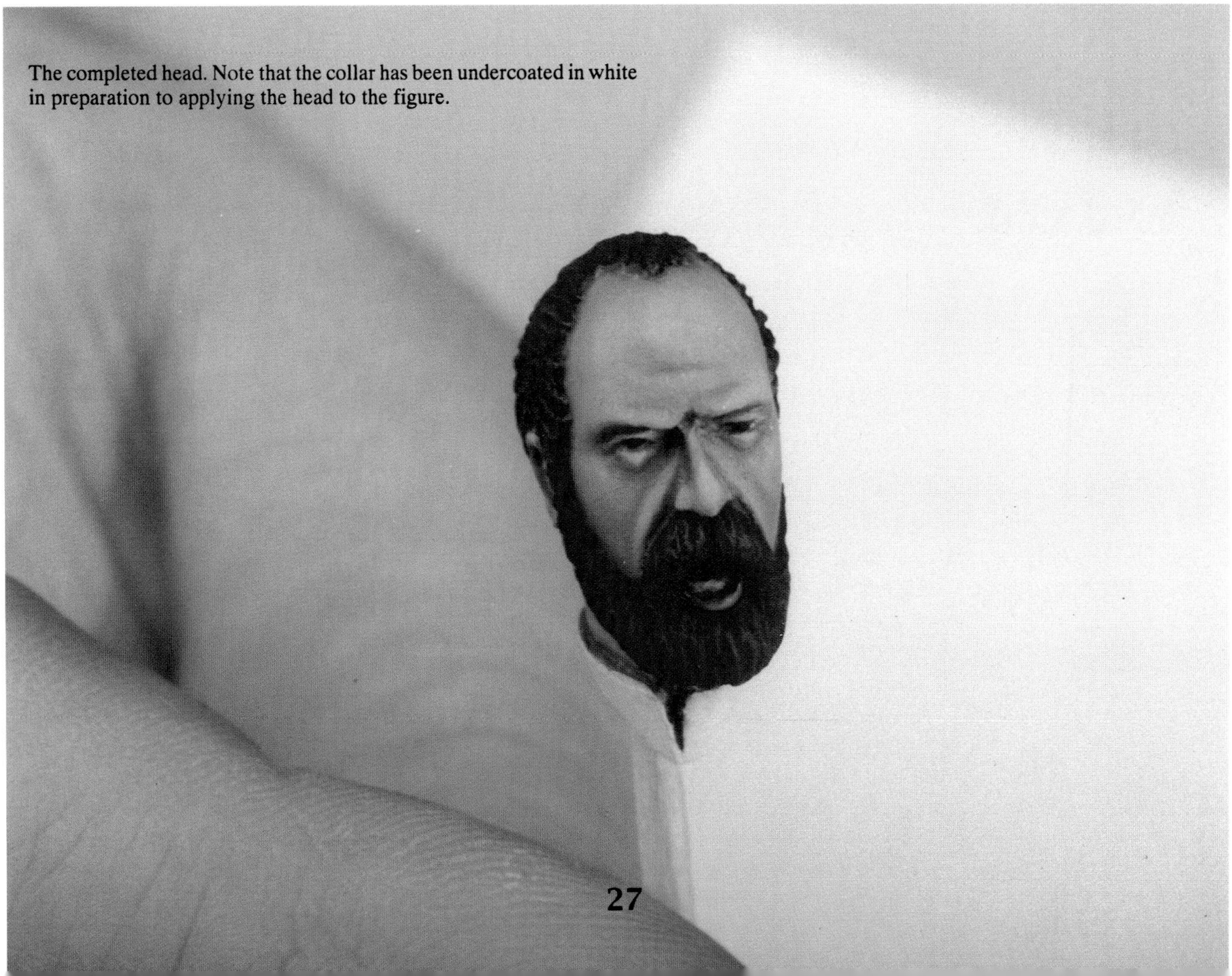

The completed head. Note that the collar has been undercoated in white in preparation to applying the head to the figure.

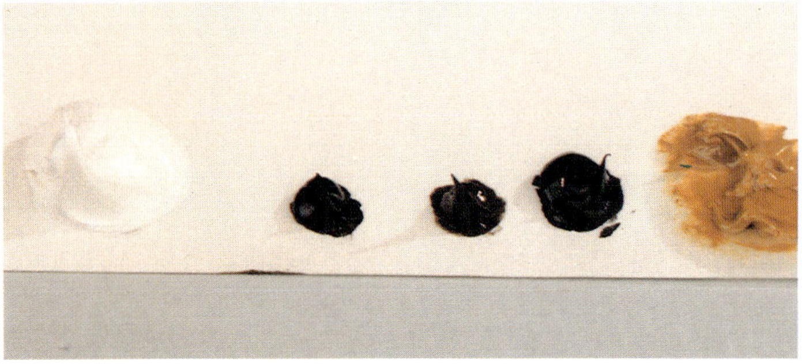

For the general's jacket, I decided to mix a gray composed of White, Black, Payne's Gray, a small amount of Yellow Ocher, and a small dab of Raw Umber. The last two colors give the gray a slightly brownish shade or earth-tone.

After mixing the five colors for the jacket together, the center shade is our basic jacket color. The darker shade is the basic jacket color with additional black and Payne's Gray added to create the shadowing color. The lighter gray spot is the basic jacket color with additional white added for our highlight color.

Apply the basic gray.

Apply the shadow color to the bottoms of folds, belt and strap outlines belts, and to the braid work as well.

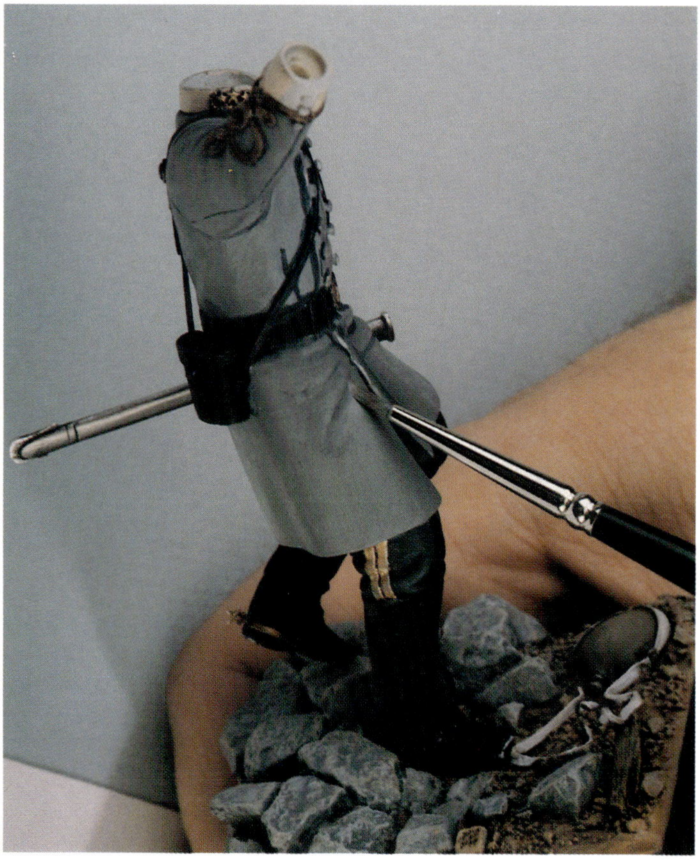

Blend and soften the basic and shadow colors.

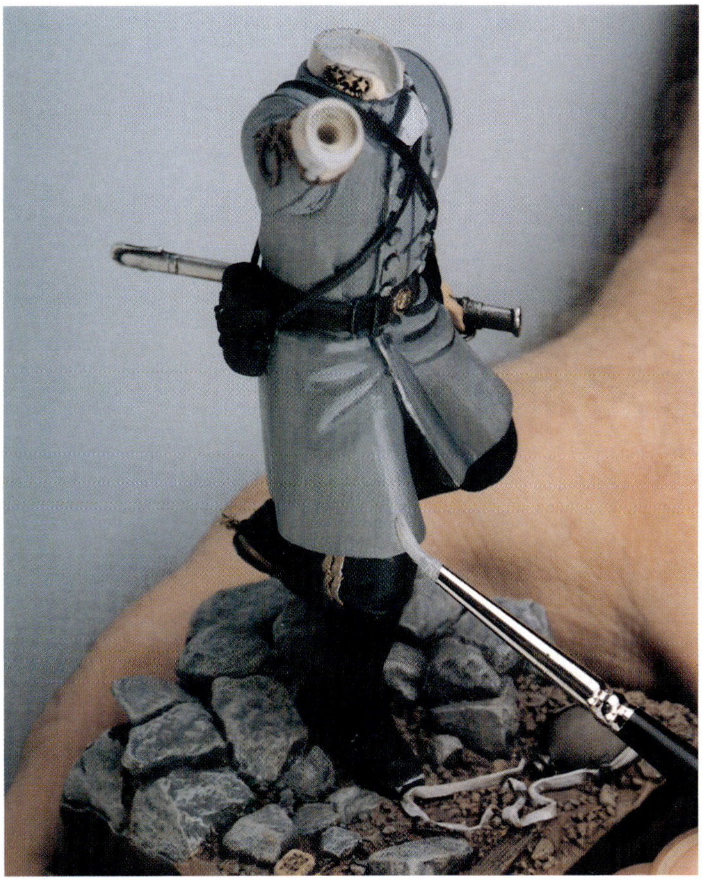

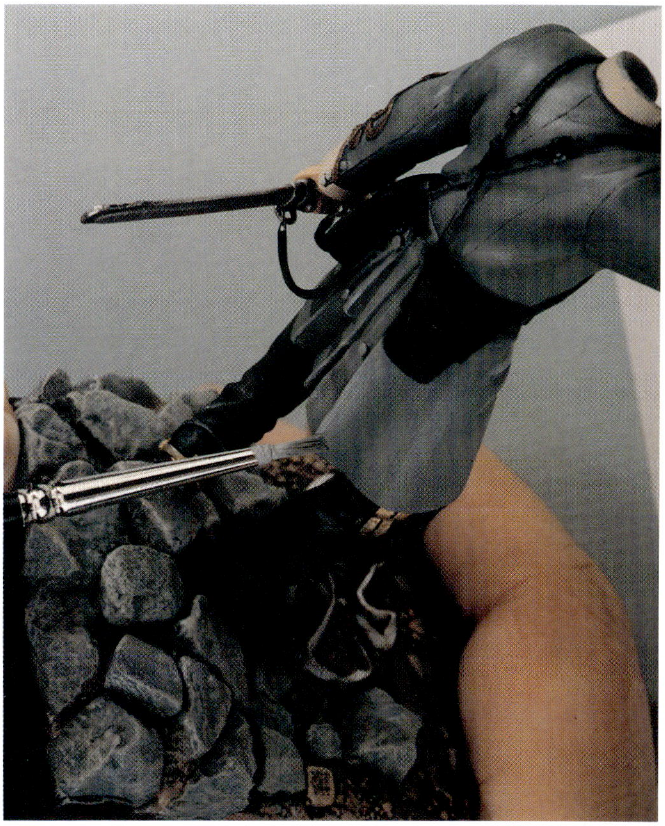

Blend the highlights. The techniques you have just used on the Confederate jacket will apply to Union uniforms as well. The colors for both Confederate and Union uniforms may be found at the back of this book.

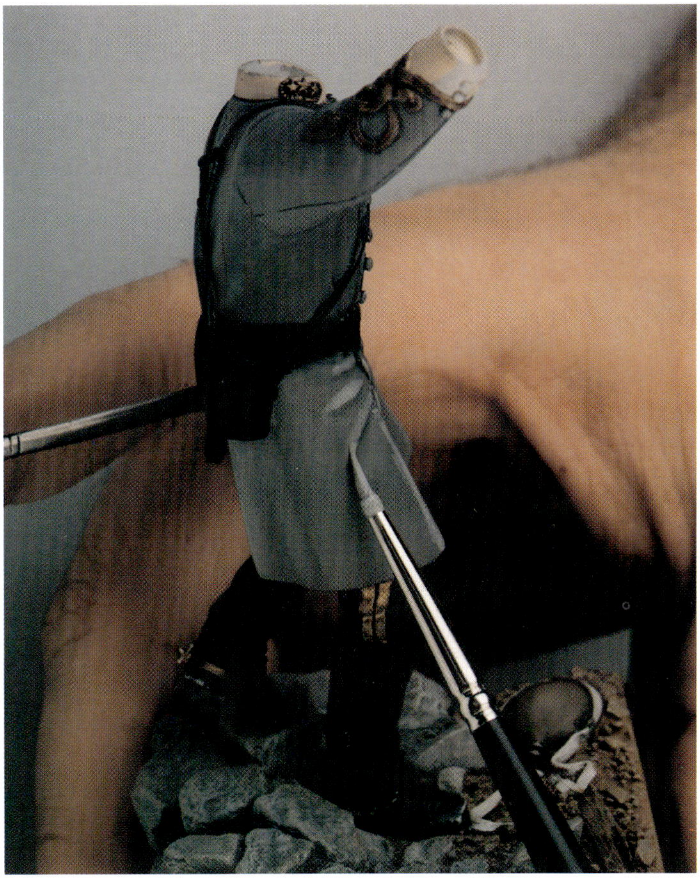

Apply the highlight color to areas that would pick up the jacket's natural highlights, such as tops of folds, shoulders, etc.

The completed jacket. Do not be overly concerned if through the blending process you get some of the jacket color on the undercoated belts and buttons. Just go back in and undercoat again where necessary.

Undercoating the belts again.

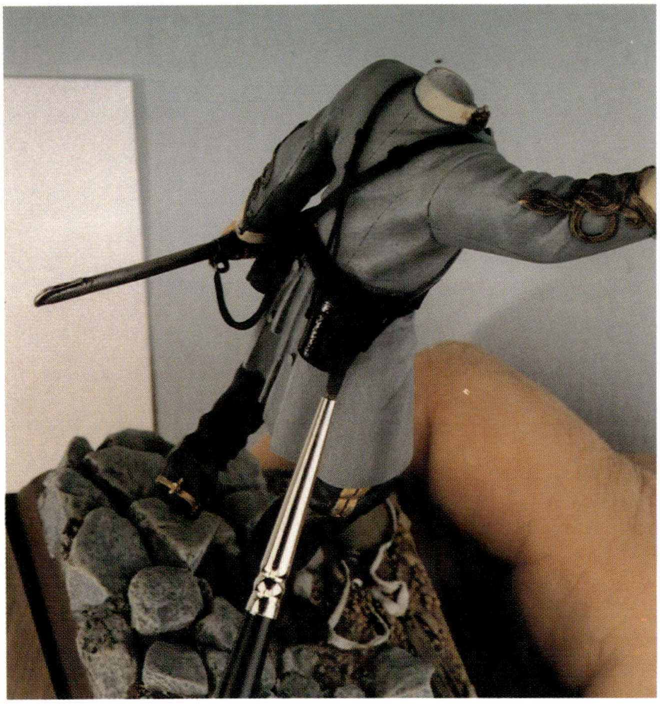

Using black artist paints, paint the binocular case, all of the straps, the haversack, and the boots. We will use this as our deep shadow color.

A dark brown such as Burnt Sienna or Mars Brown mixed with Black is used as a highlight color for black leather items.

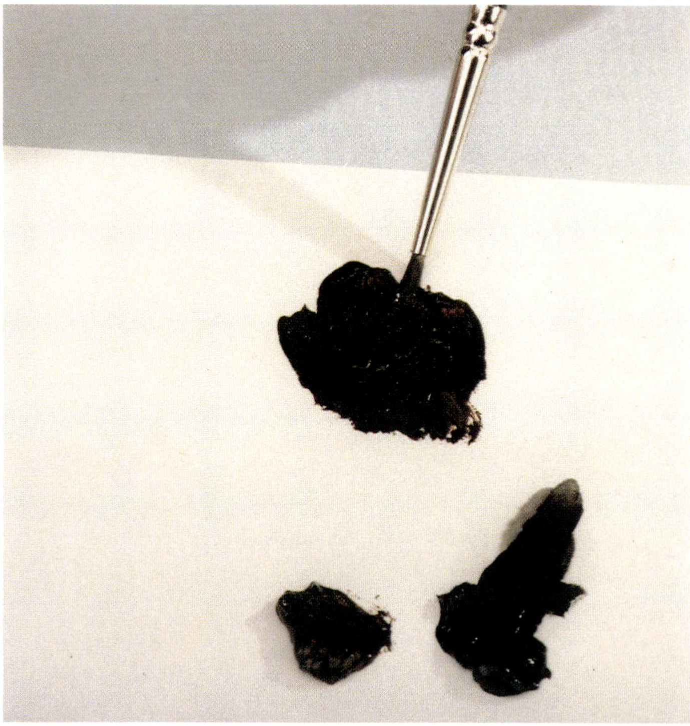

When blending, this will be a subtle change from the straight black.

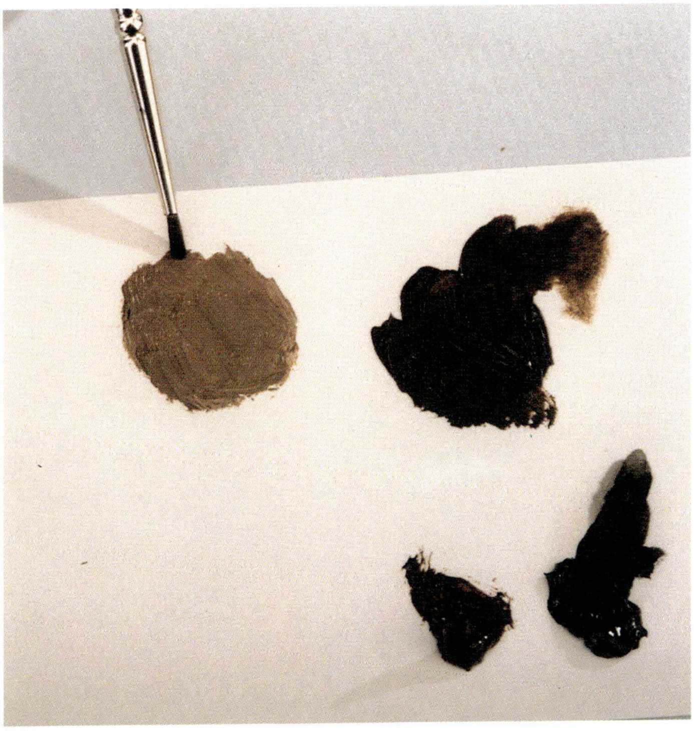

This will become our light highlight. It is a mixture of the brown and black with a small amount of white added.

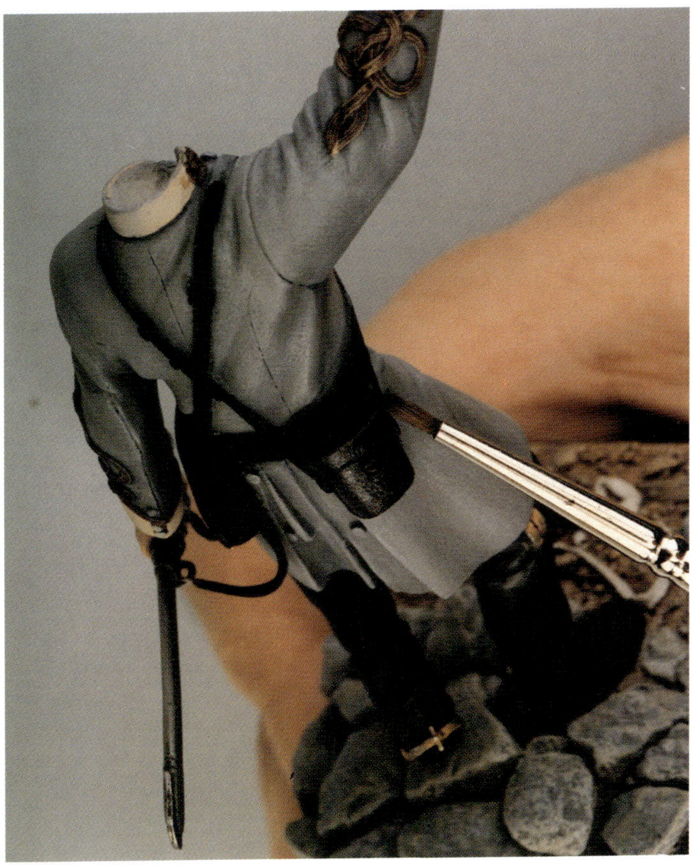

This highlight is applied to raised areas or areas of the heaviest wear to bring out the detail. A light touch needs to be used to insure that the black items do not become too brown. Black is a color which can easily shade into brown or gray if too much of another color is applied.

For boots, you can add an even higher highlight to add more wear and to create a dust effect. Be careful to put this highlight only on the areas of extreme wear.

The completed boots. Note the areas highlighted to show extreme wear.

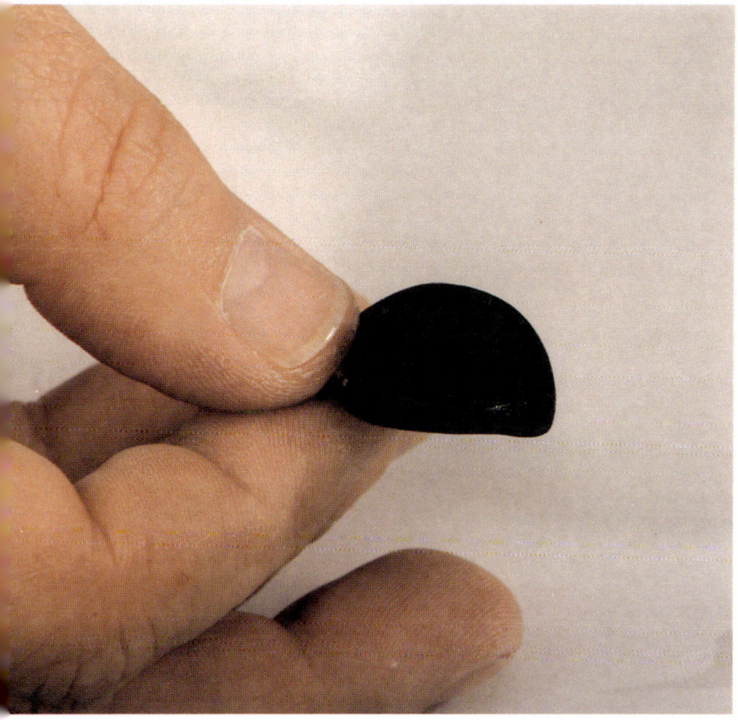

I have undercoated the hat with black hobby paint.

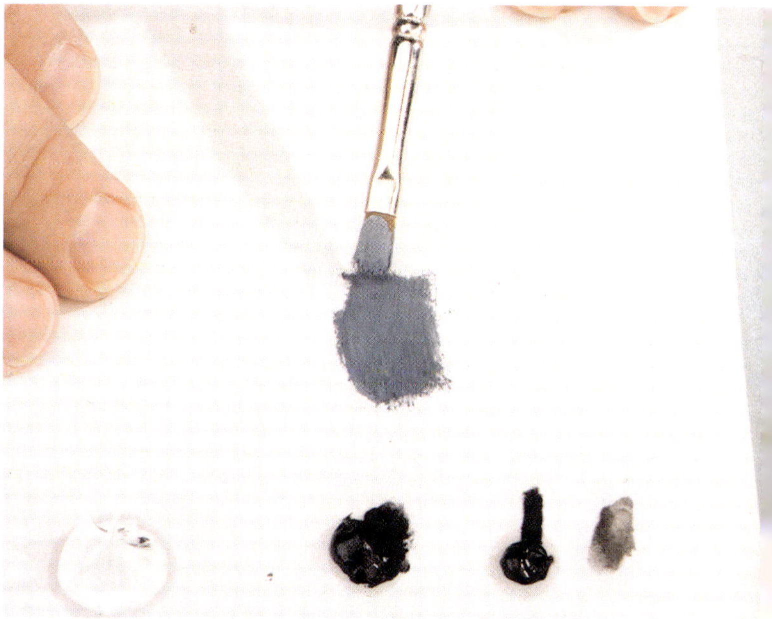

I mix Payne's Gray & White together to arrive at this first highlight color. I like to use grays and blue grays to highlight black cloth items instead of the brownish highlights for black leather. You can also use black and white mixed together to achieve the highlight color instead of gray.

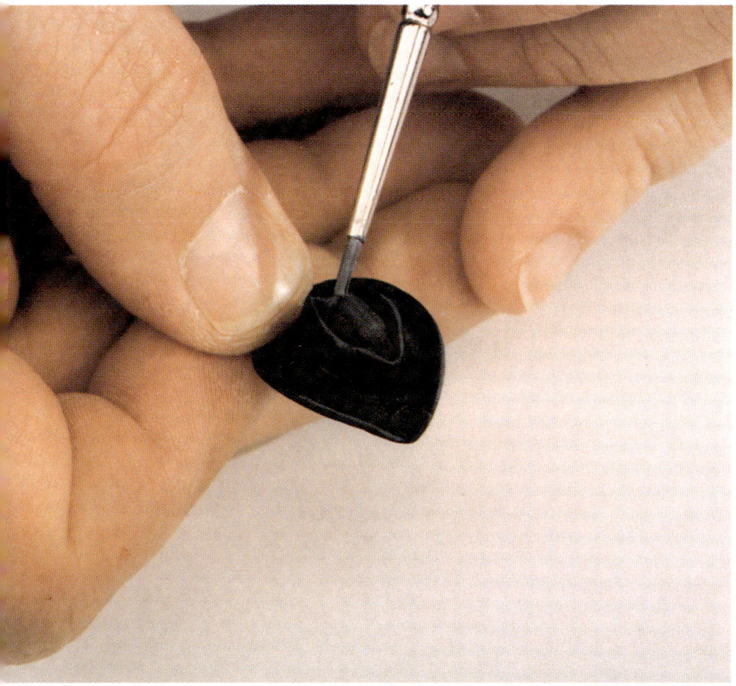

I then cover the entire hat with Ivory Black oil paint.

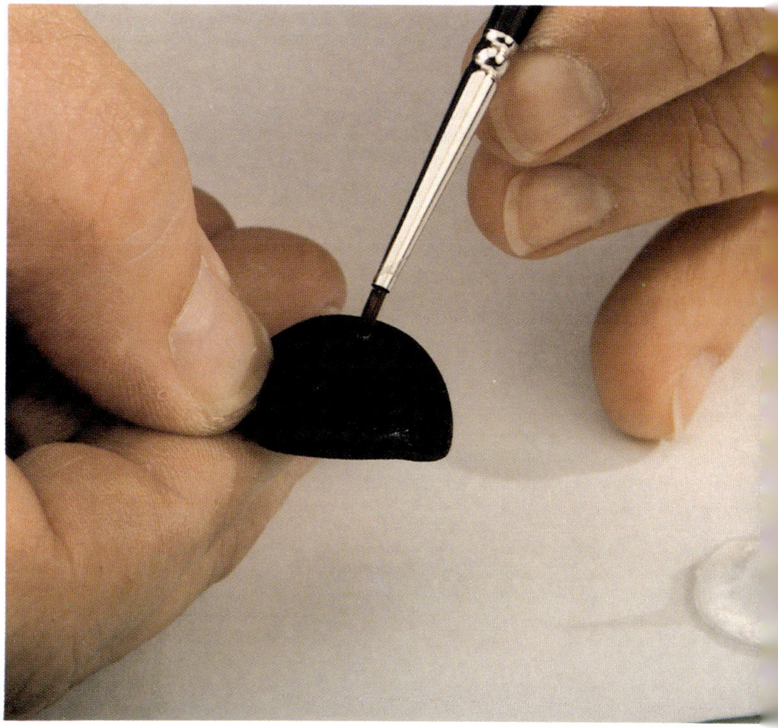

Place the highlight tint on all raised areas, being careful not to drag it into the recesses.

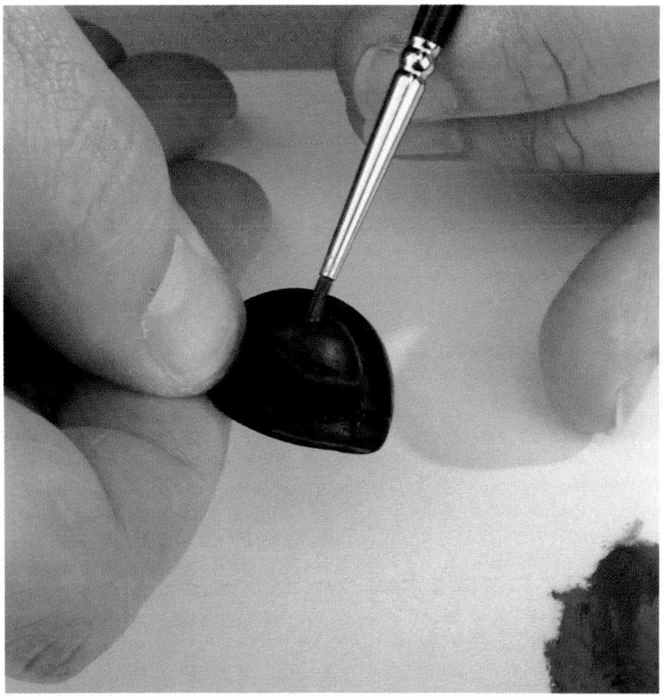

Blend the edges of the highlight to soften the transition between the two colors.

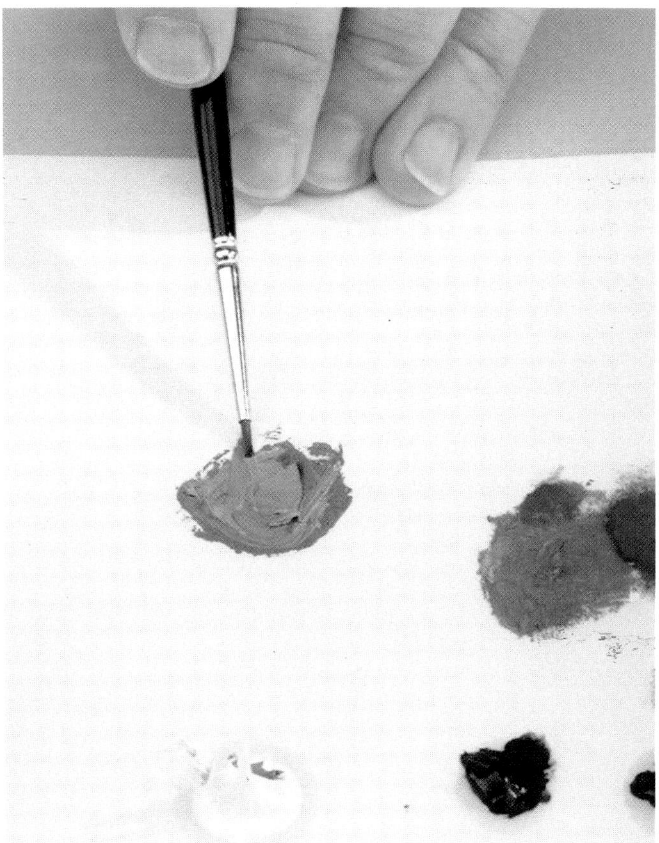

Adding additional white to the first highlight color, we arrive at the final highlight tint.

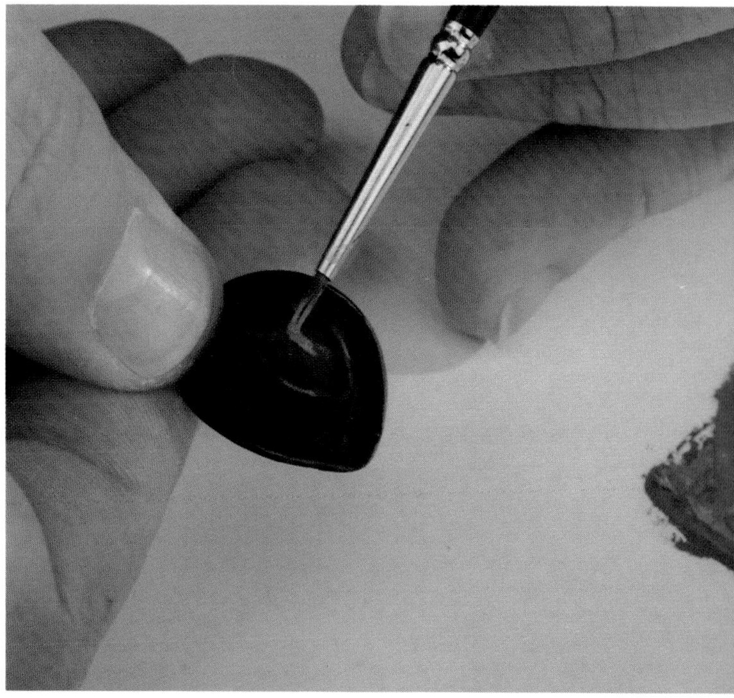

This tint is applied and blended into only to the highest parts of the raised areas.

The finished hat.

Using the flesh that I mixed for the face, I now paint the hands. I didn't paint the hands at the same time as the face because I wanted to attach them to the figure before painting. Applying the shadows.

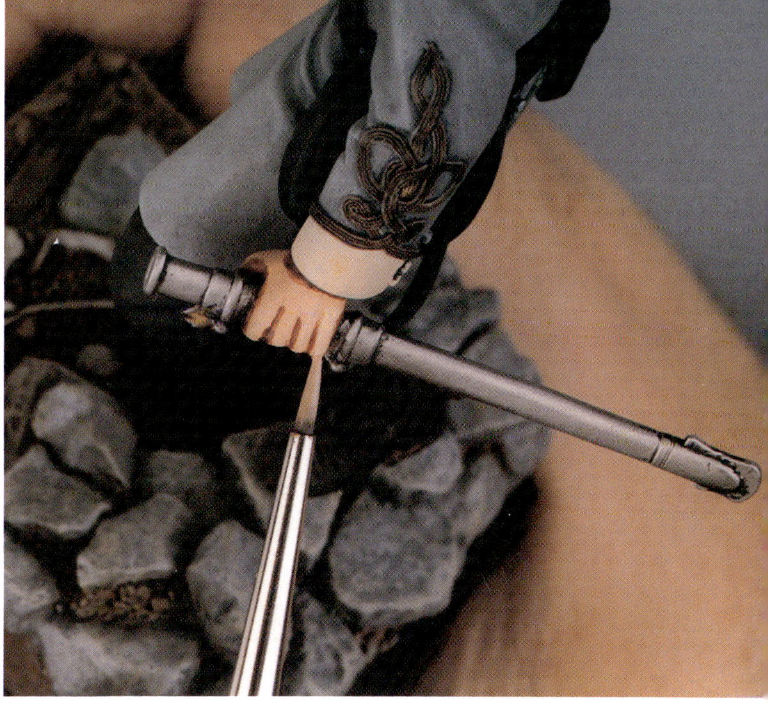

Next, I apply the middle flesh tone to the rest of the hand.

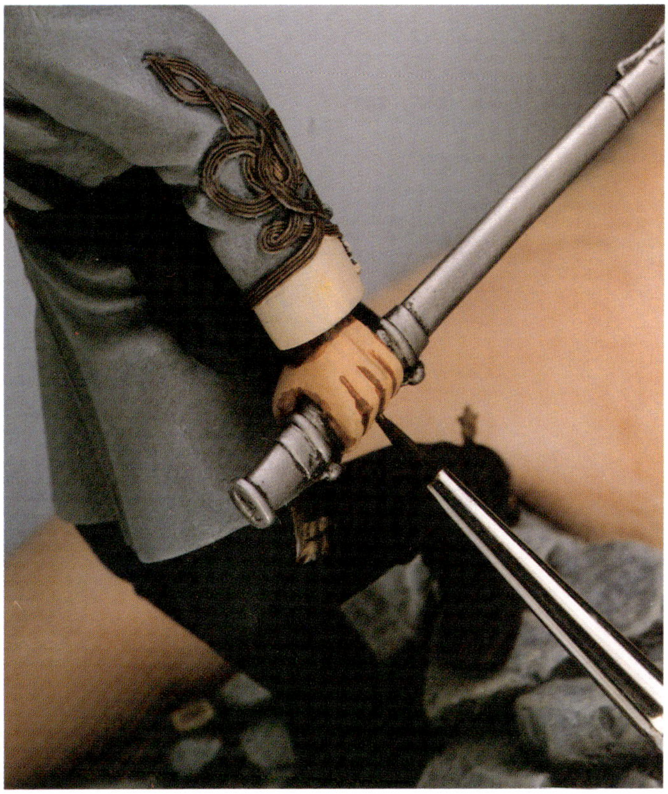

I begin painting the undercoated hands with Burnt Sienna staying in the deeper recesses such as between the fingers, where the wrist meets the jacket, where the hand touches the scabbard.

Blend the colors together and soften the edges between the two.

The blended hand.

Blend the transition areas between the flesh tone and its highlight.

I now add the highlights to the raised areas on the hand, including the knuckles of the fingers and the tendons on the back of the hand.

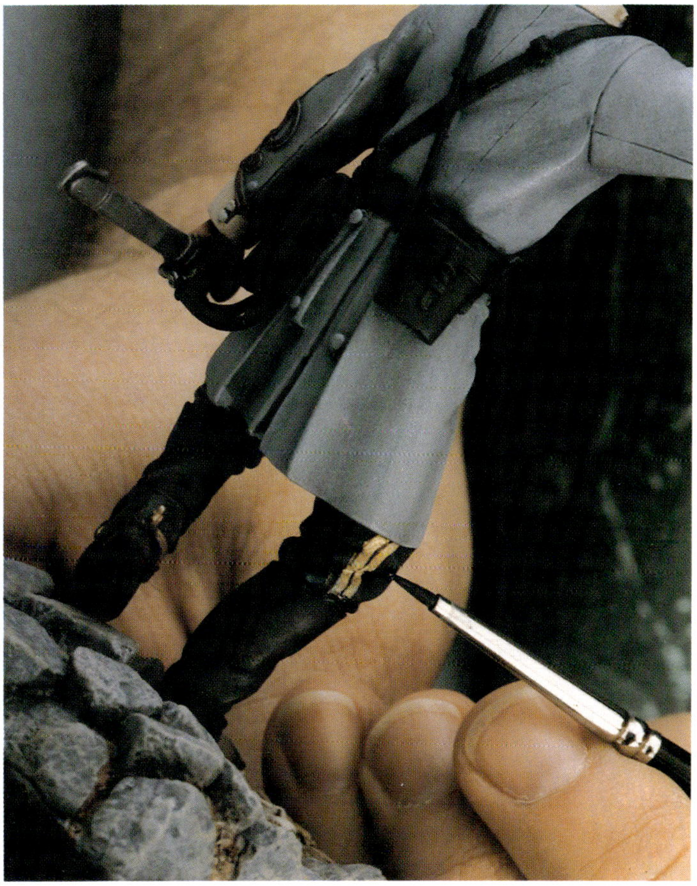

Begin painting the dark blue pants by putting Ivory Black into the deepest recesses. This serves as the shadow color. Incidentally, this is exactly the way I paint Federal Blue when painting Union uniforms.

Completed hands.

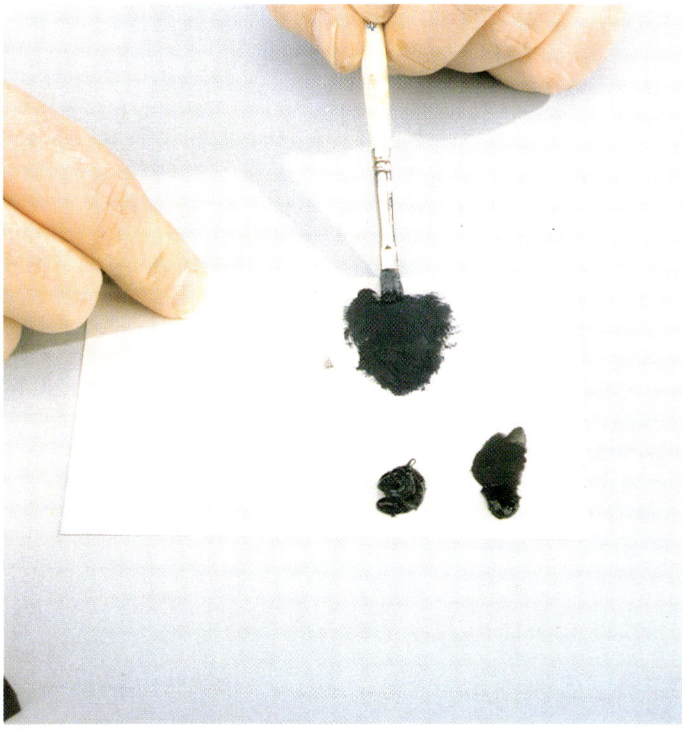

The blue for the pants (the middle color) is mixed by adding a small amount of black and white to indigo. Be sure to keep the mixture dark.

Applying the mixed blue to the areas that were not covered by the shadow color.

Add more white to the middle color to create a slightly lighter shade.

Blend these colors.

Place this color at the tops of the folds, on the knees ... any place that would pick up highlights.

Carefully blend these colors.

I am adding a little bit of Yellow Ocher to the blue. This will be applied to the knees to imply dirt.

For gold braid work, I first paint it dark brown with a thin layer of hobby paint. Let this dry completely.

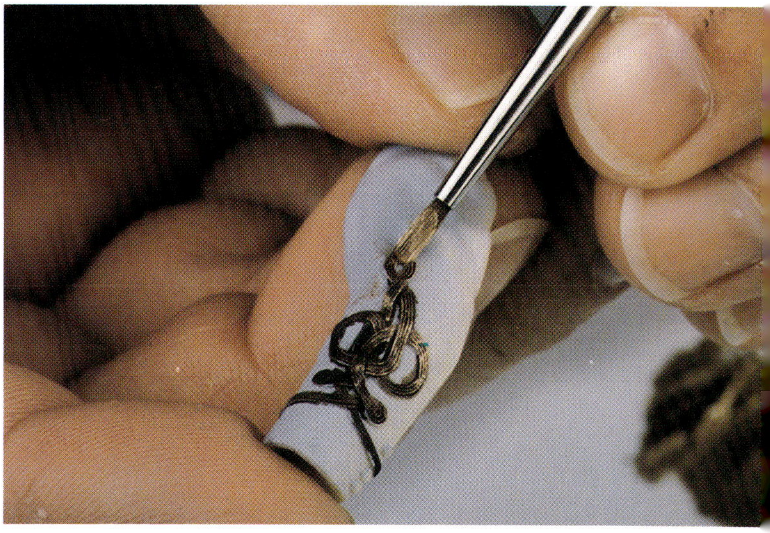

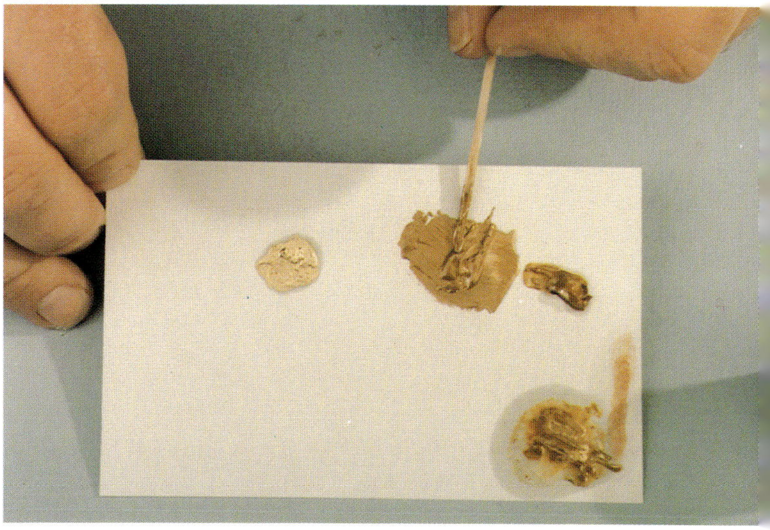

I then apply hobby gold or gold and yellow ocher in the same manner as we highlighted the rocks on the base, lightly pick out the details while leaving the brown in the crevices to show detail. If you prefer a less "metallic" finish, add yellow ocher to the gold. Keep in mind that gold lace has a dull finish.
Lightly applying the gold to areas of the lace.

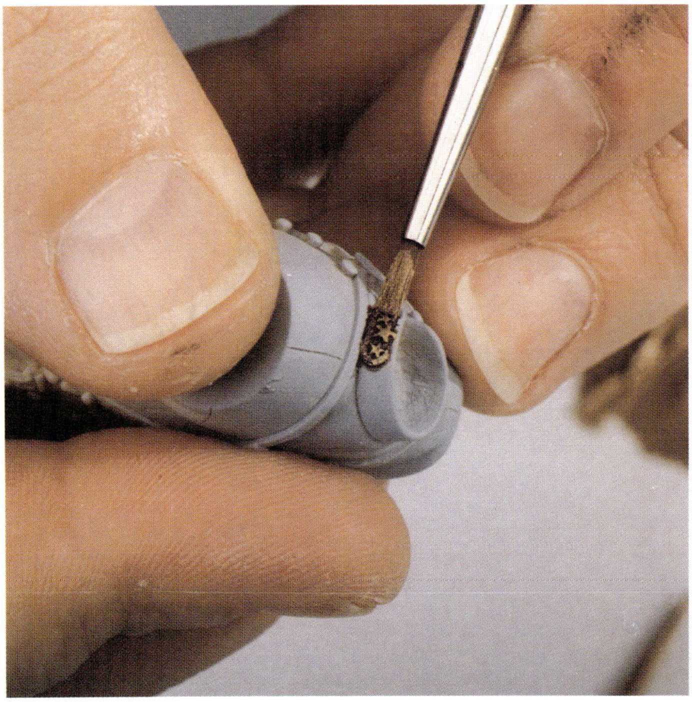

Continue applying this gold to the rank insignias on the collar ...

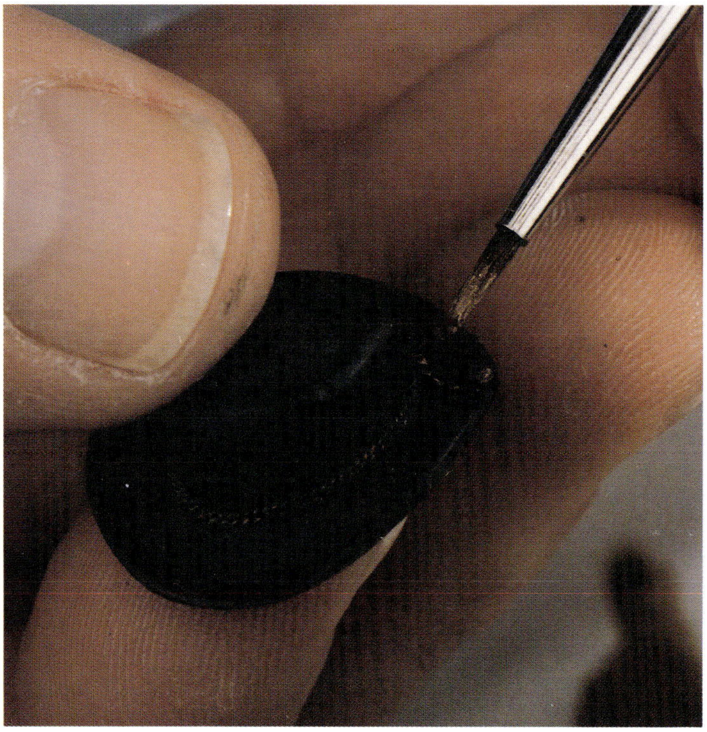

Apply gold to the cap cord as well.

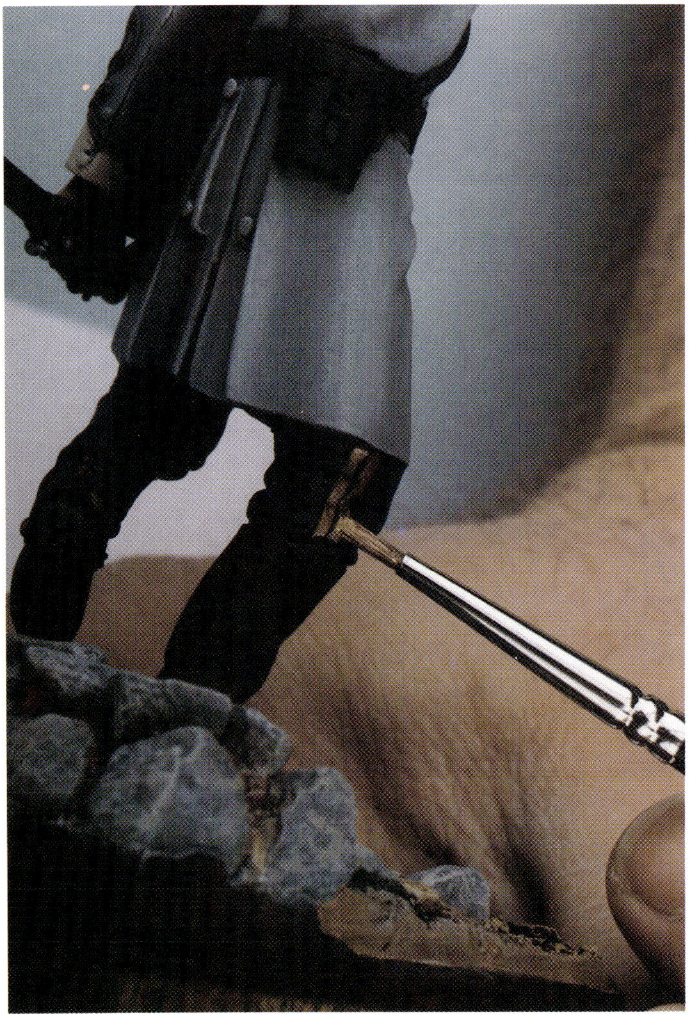

... and on the stripes on the trousers.

The finished braid work on the sleeve.

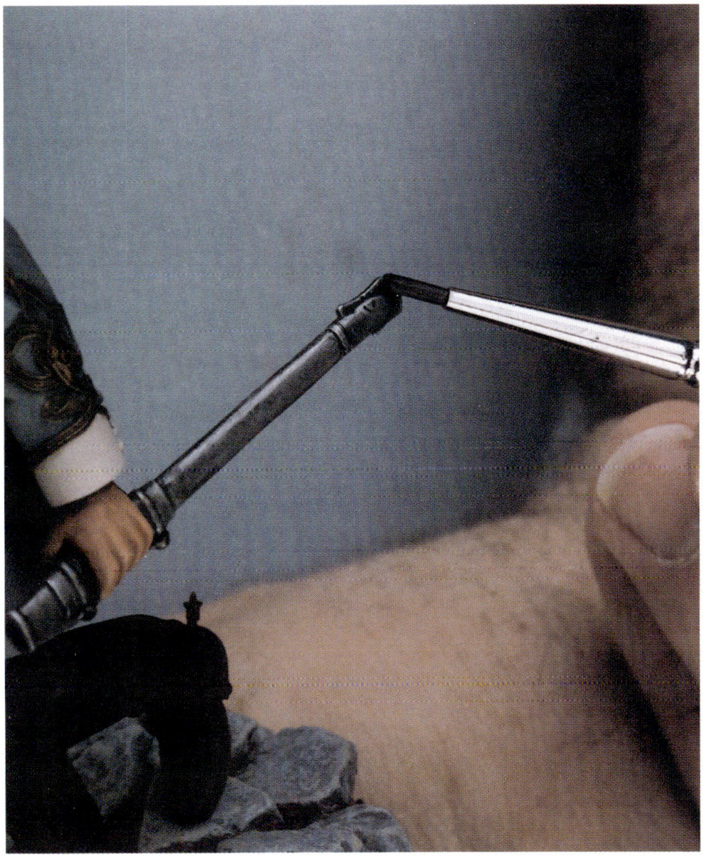

Return to the burnished metal parts. After burnishing, mix up a thin wash of black paint and let it flow into the recessed areas of the polished metal.

Let this black wash dry thoroughly and then carefully wipe the burnished areas with a soft cloth to wipe off the excess.

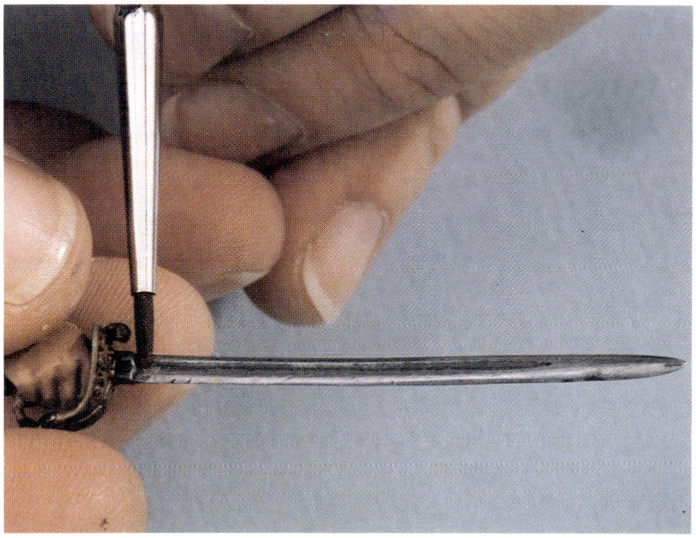

Applying black wash to the sword.

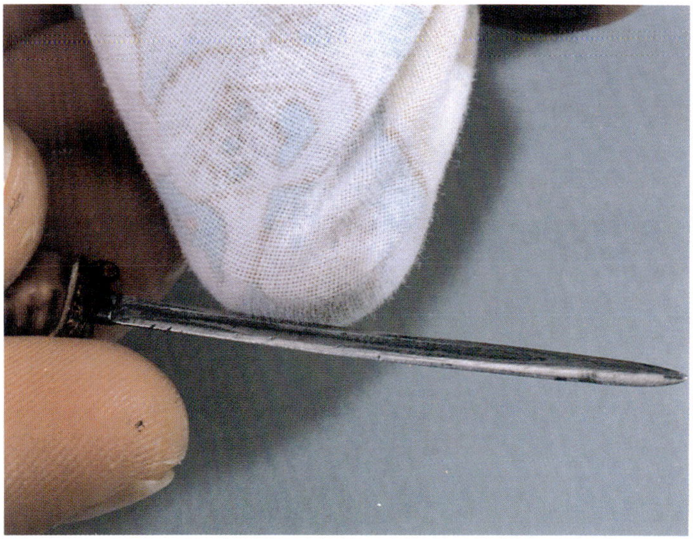

Polishing the sword.

To keep the metal from dulling or tarnishing, apply a coat of clear gloss.

The finished scabba

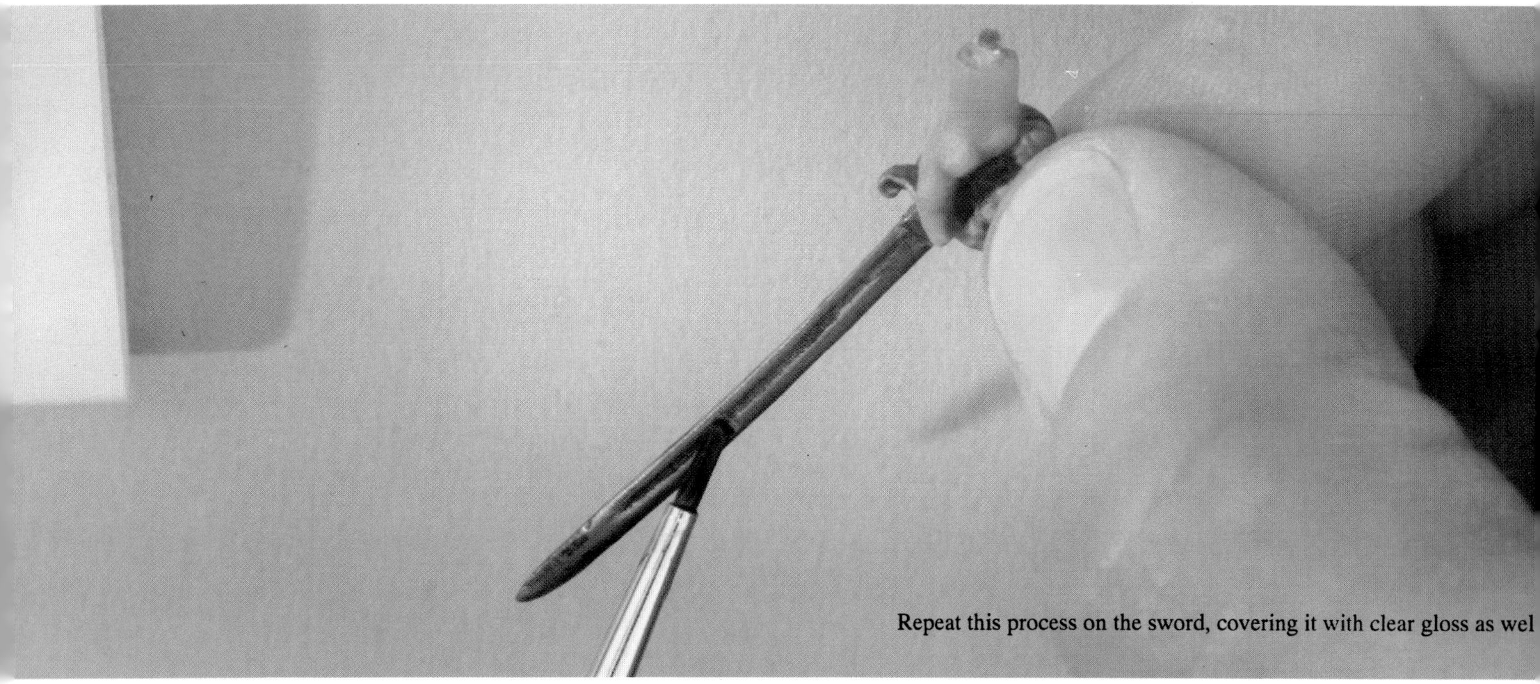

Repeat this process on the sword, covering it with clear gloss as wel

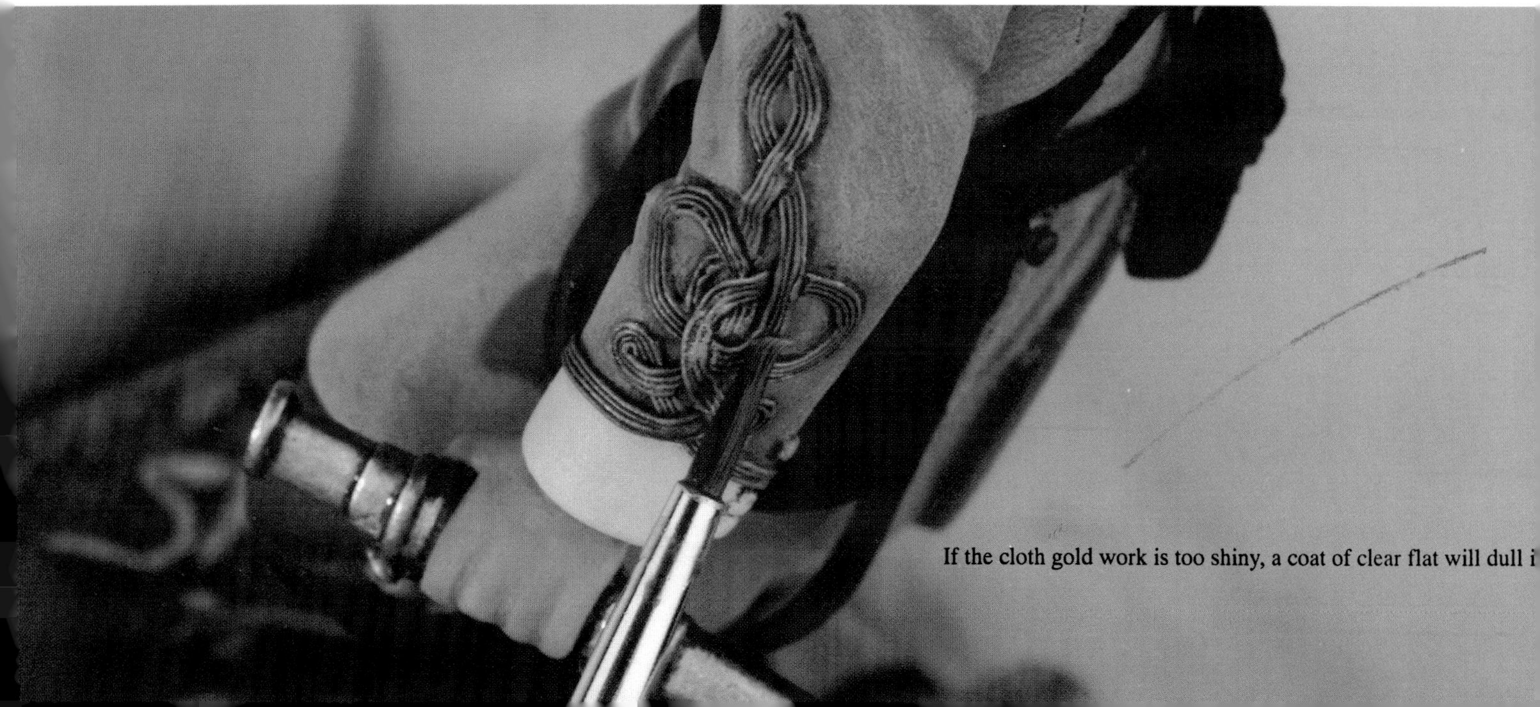

If the cloth gold work is too shiny, a coat of clear flat will dull i

The dulled pants stripe and braid.

The dulled stripe.

For gold metal parts, such as buttons, buckles, and the hilt of the sword, I again paint these items dark brown first.

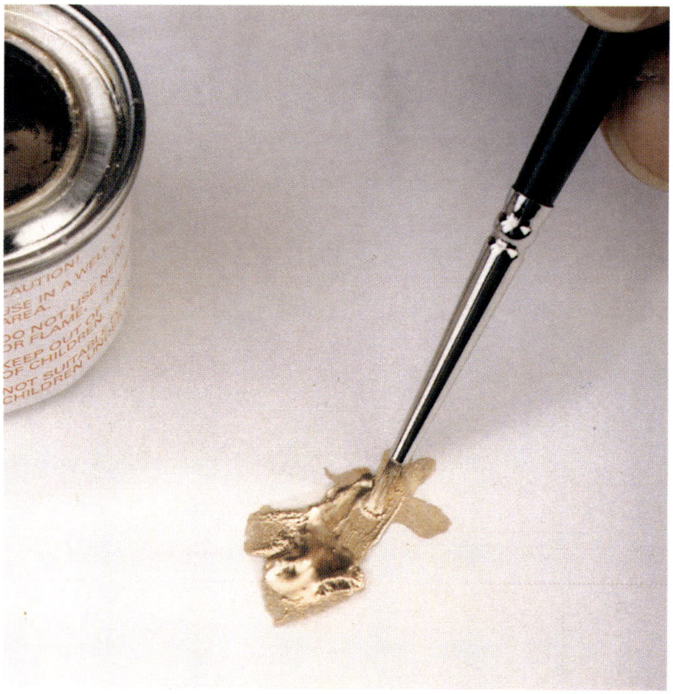

Using the clear fluid at the top, I then thin my gold paint to a workable consistency.

Then I use gold hobby paint. I don't shake my metallic paints. I use a toothpick and pull up some of the pigment at the bottom of the can. This gives me a very strong metallic color.

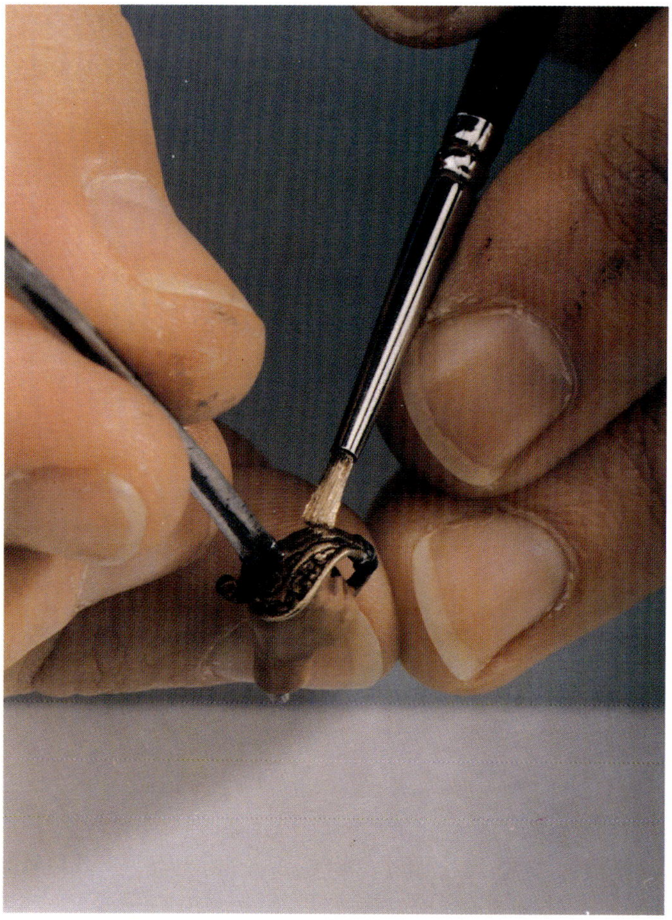

For metal objects with carved relief (such as sword hilts and belt buckles) I use the same dry brush techniques as I used on the rocks — lightly picking out the raised detail on the sword hilt ...

... and on the belt buckle.

On most buttons you really can't pick out any details. Just paint them gold.

Don't forget the buttons on the back of the jacket ...

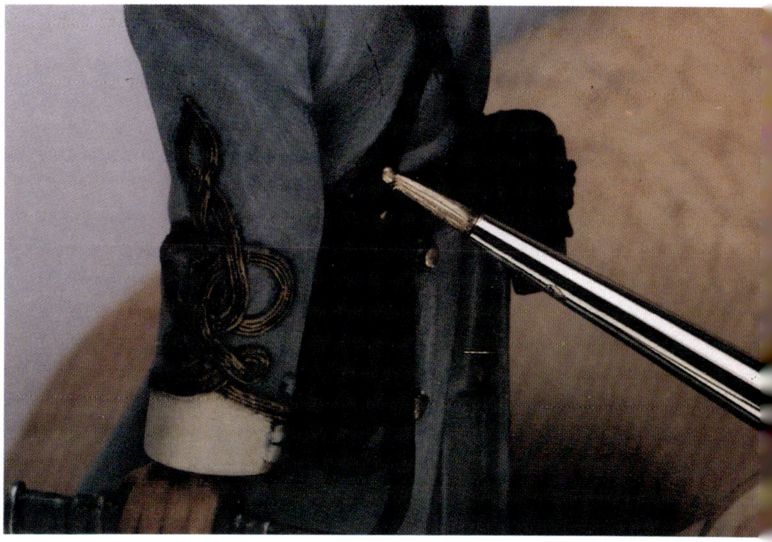

... or the small details including attachment rings on the equipment, ...

... any buckles, ...

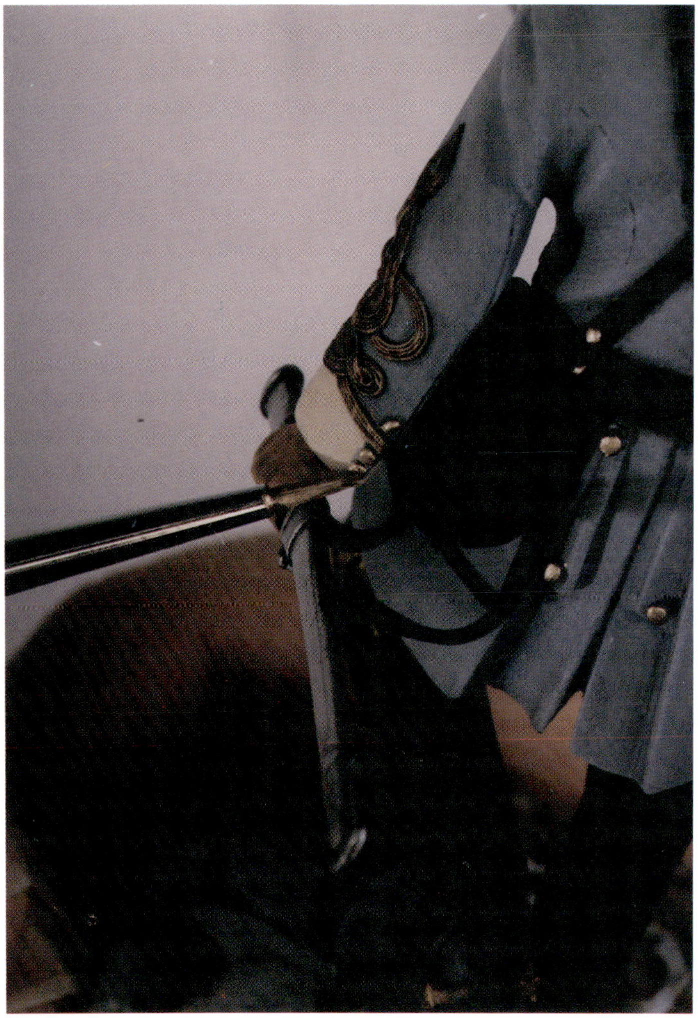

... buttons on the sleeves, ...

... and spurs.

The painted buttons, front and back. Buckle details are visible on the back as well.

PLACE
STAMP
HERE

SCHIFFER PUBLISHING LTD
77 LOWER VALLEY RD
ATGLEN PA 19310-9717

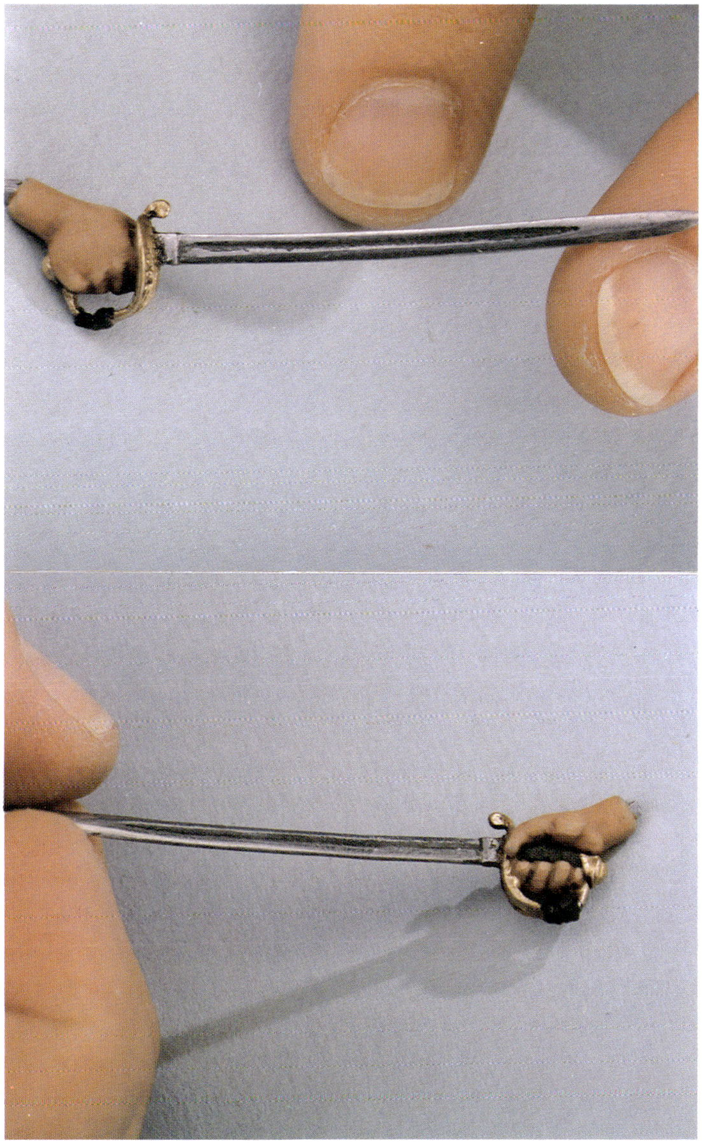

The completed sword hilt. On the reverse of the sword hilt, notice that the handle and part of the sword knot have been painted black.

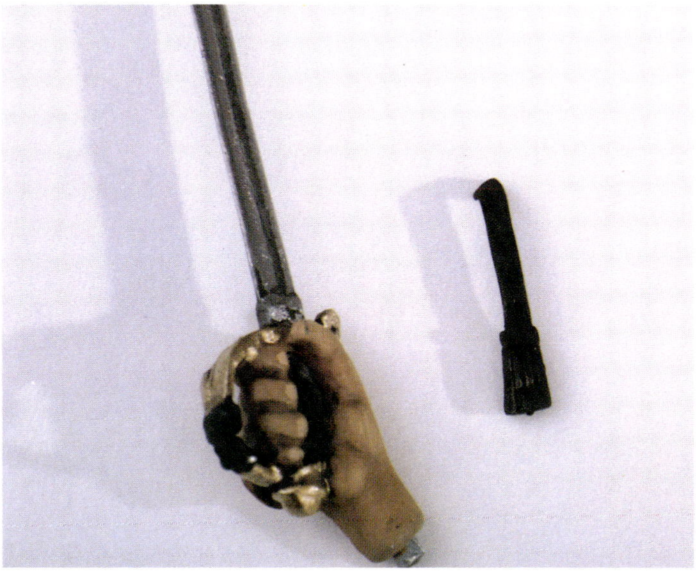

The primed and undercoated sword knot.

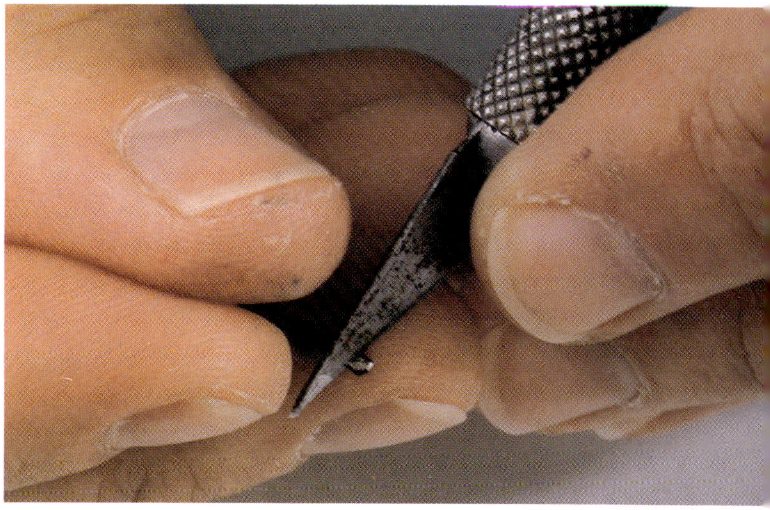

Clean off any primer or paint from the surfaces to be glued.

Apply a drop of quick drying glue to the cleaned surface of the sword knot.

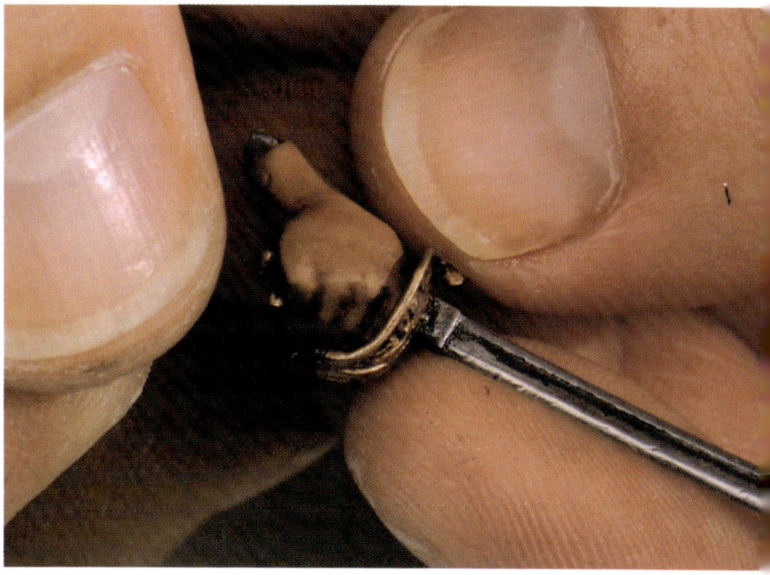

Apply the knot to the sword.

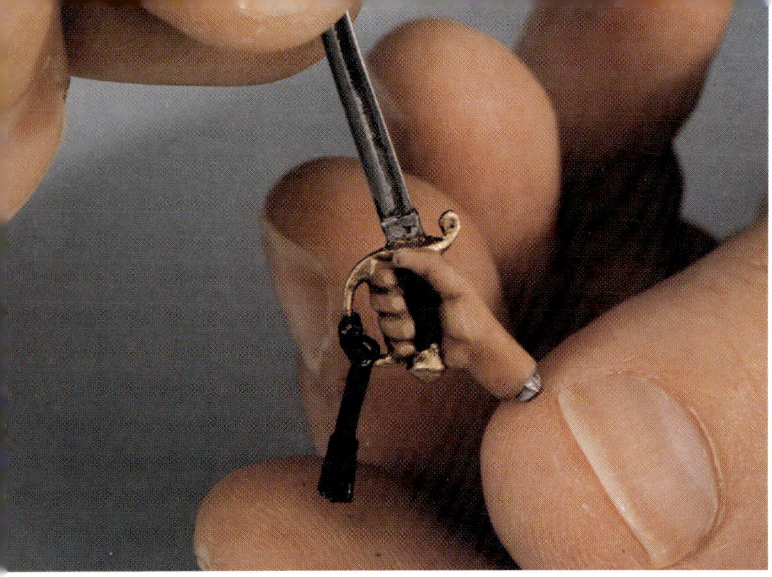

Check the knot for proper alignment.

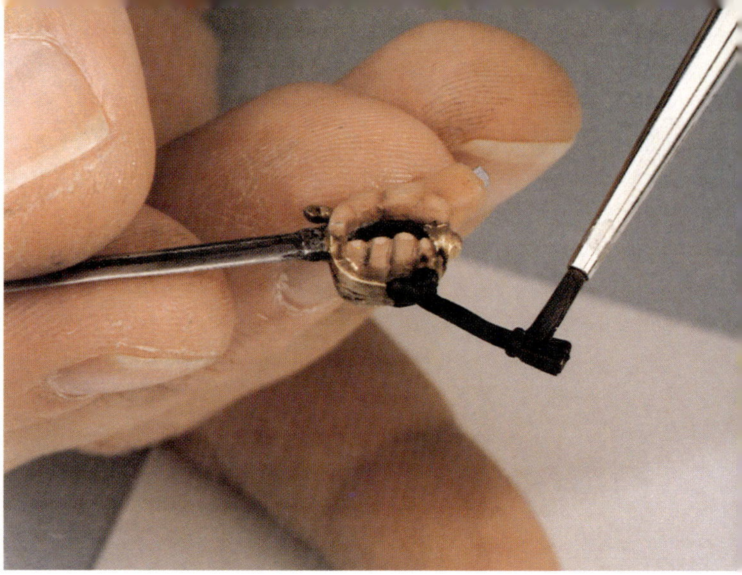

On the end of the sword knot, we apply this color using the same dry brush technique that we have used previously.

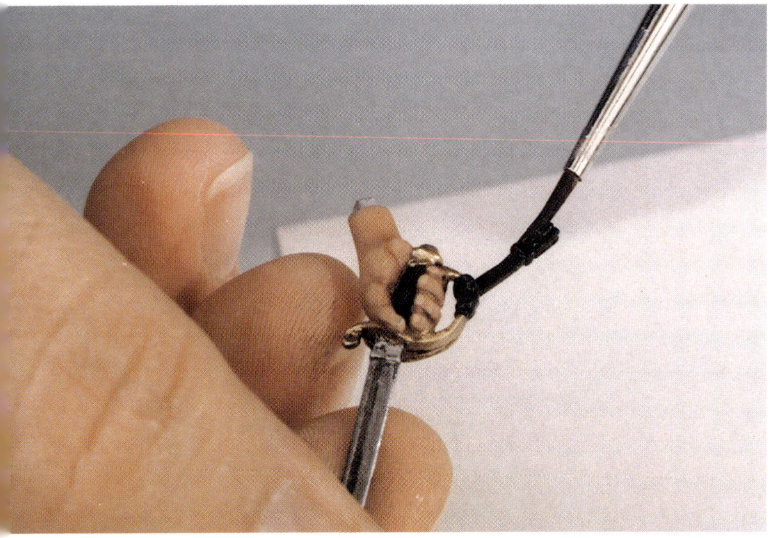

Paint the knot black with a thin coat of artist oils.

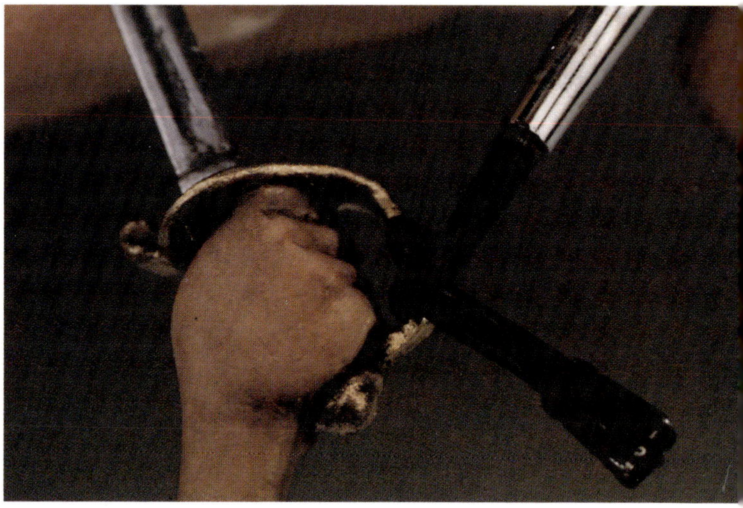

Continue on up the edges of the sword knot, picking up the details as the knot wraps around the handle of the sword.

For the middle highlight color mix a small amount of Black and Yellow Ocher together.

To the highlight color add a small amount of Yellow Ocher for a light highlight shade.

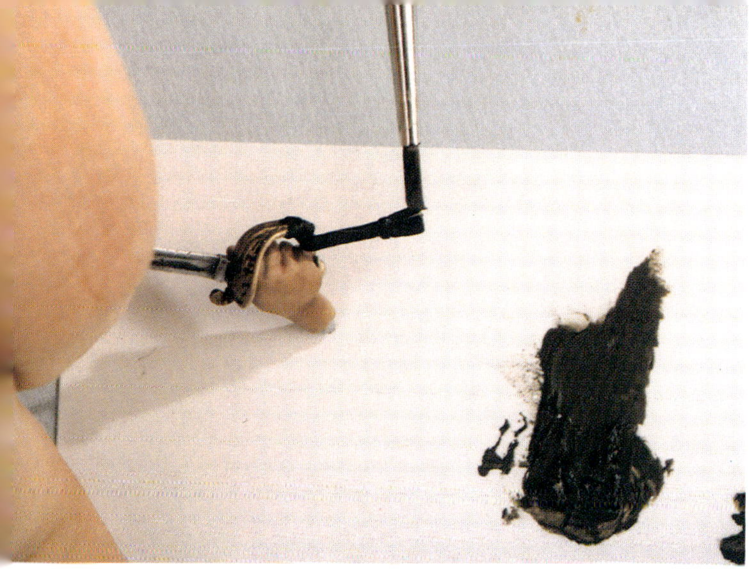

Being selective on placement, pick out the highest points on the sword knot and apply this light highlight color. Again, keep in mind you must keep this all very dark to insure that the black sword knot remains black.

The cuffs and collar for this figure are buff. This is a slightly off white color. I mixed equal amounts of Yellow Ocher and White together to create the shadow color.

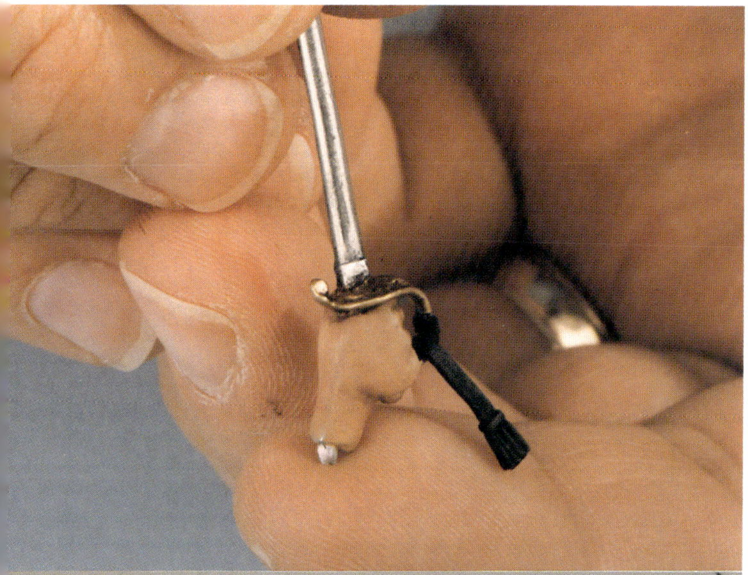

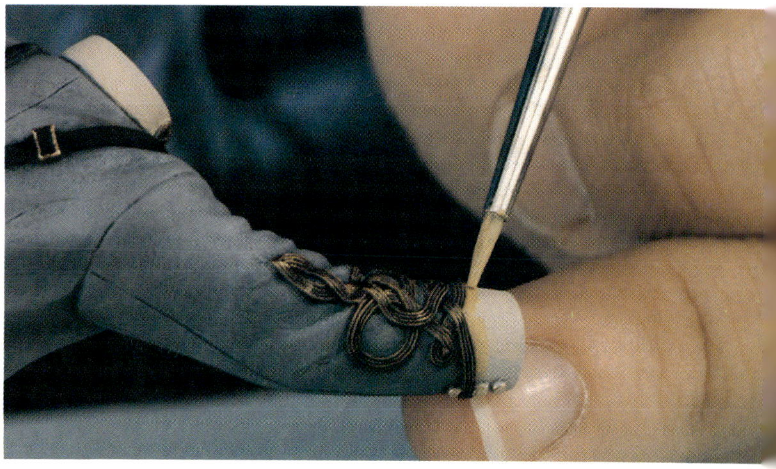

Apply this shadow color where the gold lace meets the cuff.

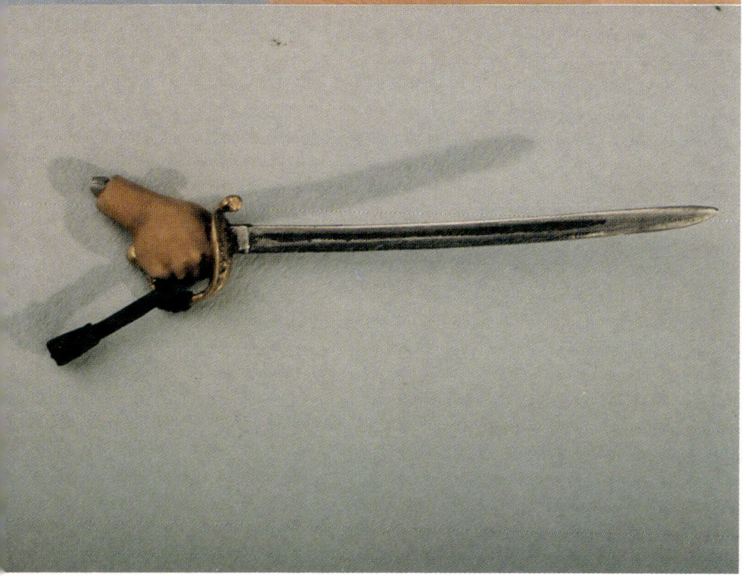

The completed sword knot and sword. We will attach this item to the arm after we have painted the cuffs and collar of the figure.

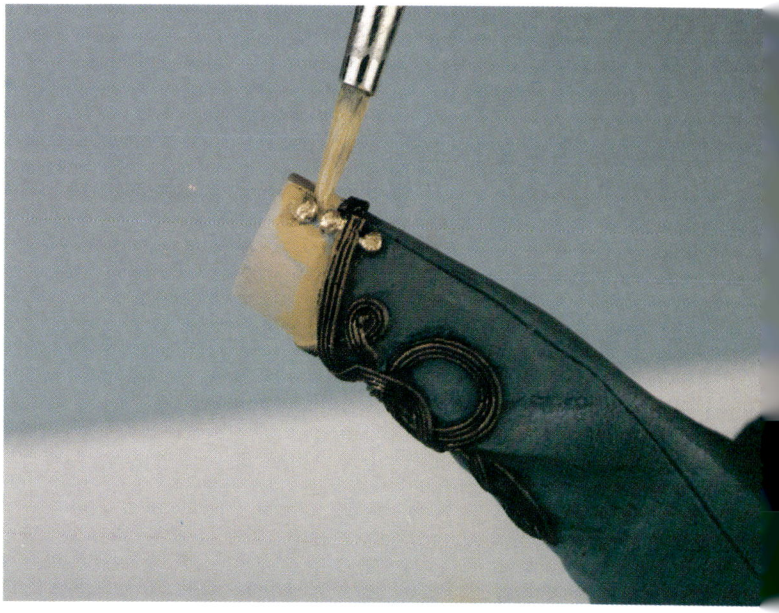

Add shadow around the buttons of the cuff as well.

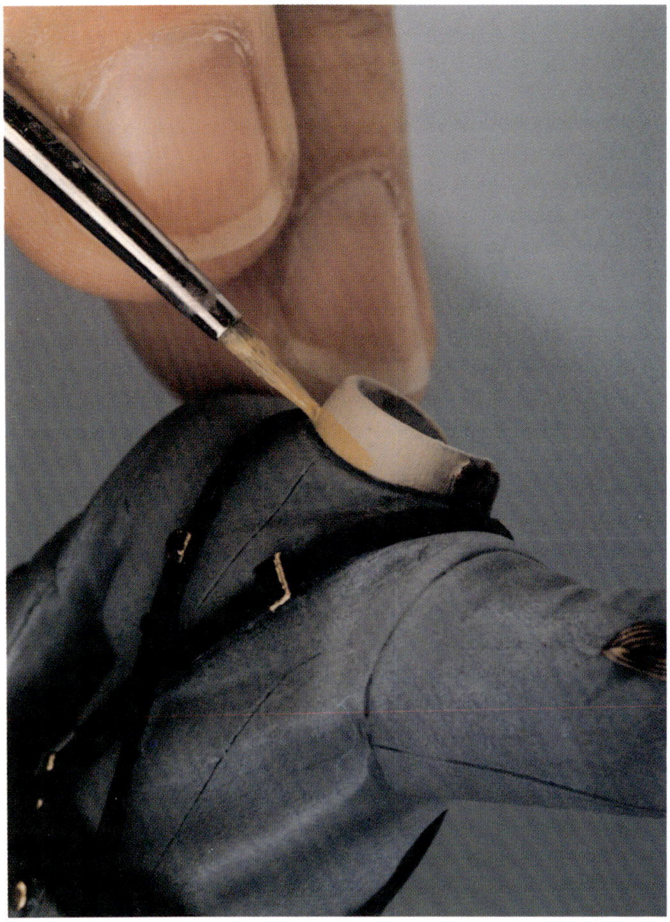

Also apply this shadow where the collar meets the jacket and around the collar insignias.

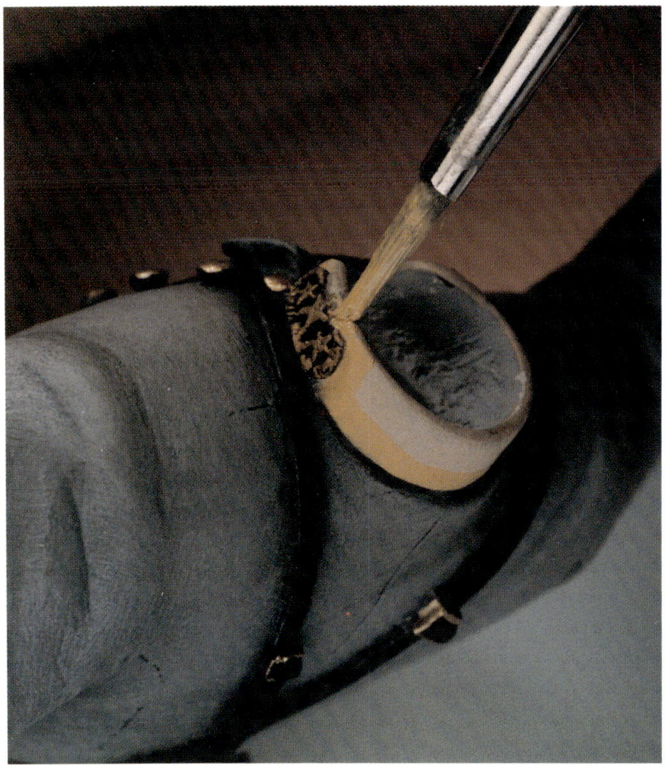

Applying shadows around the insignias.

I made a lighter shade of the dark buff to apply to the rest of the collar.

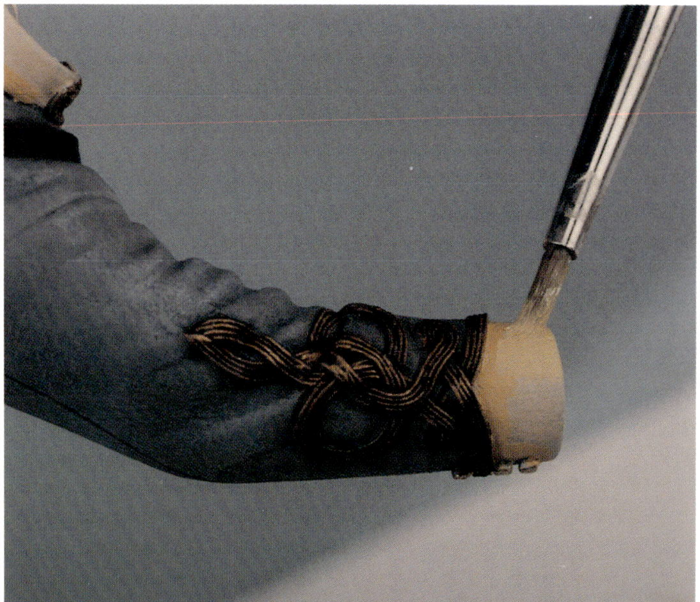

Apply this middle color to the remaining areas on the cuff and collar and then blend to soften the edges where the two colors meet.

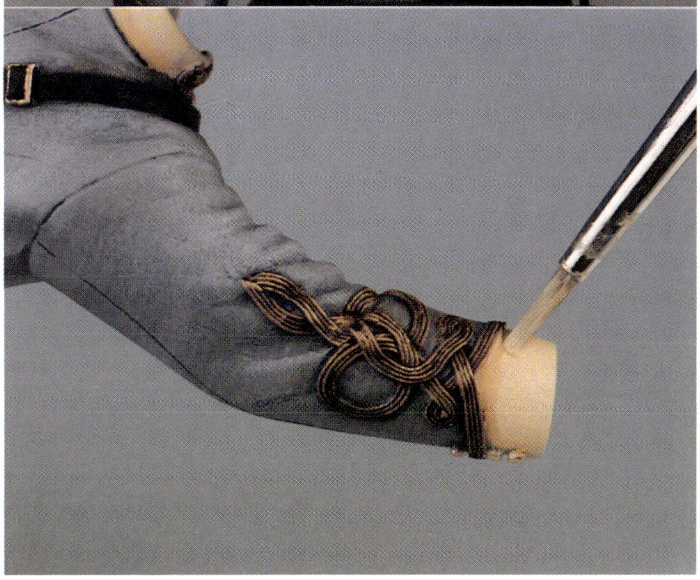

Blending the collar and the cuffs.

I have used white for my light highlight on the collar and cuffs.

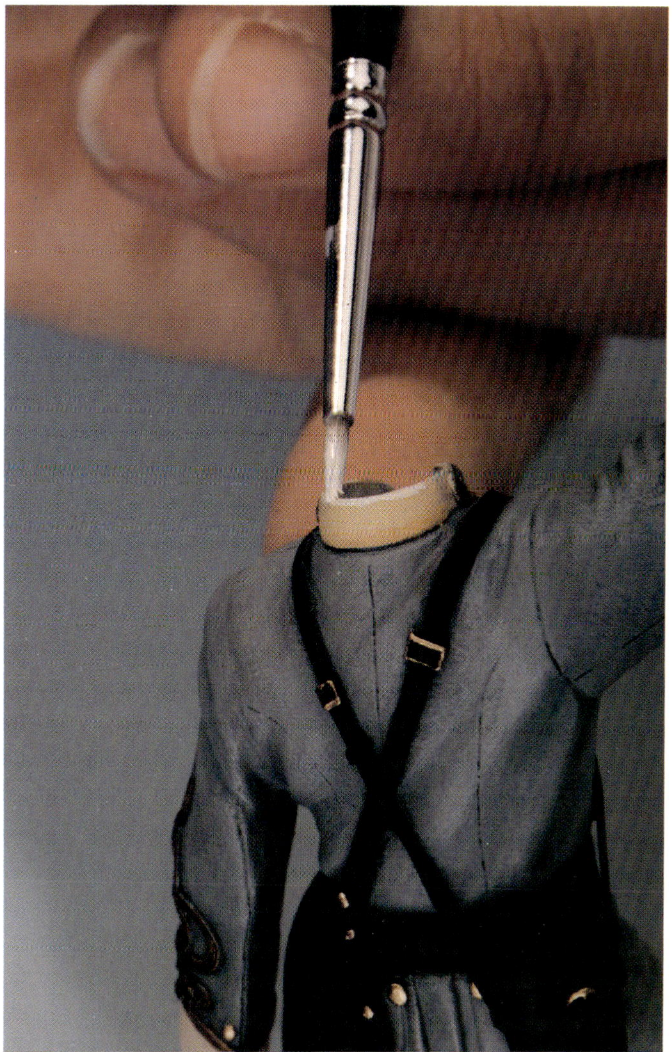

Applying white highlight to the collar and cuffs.

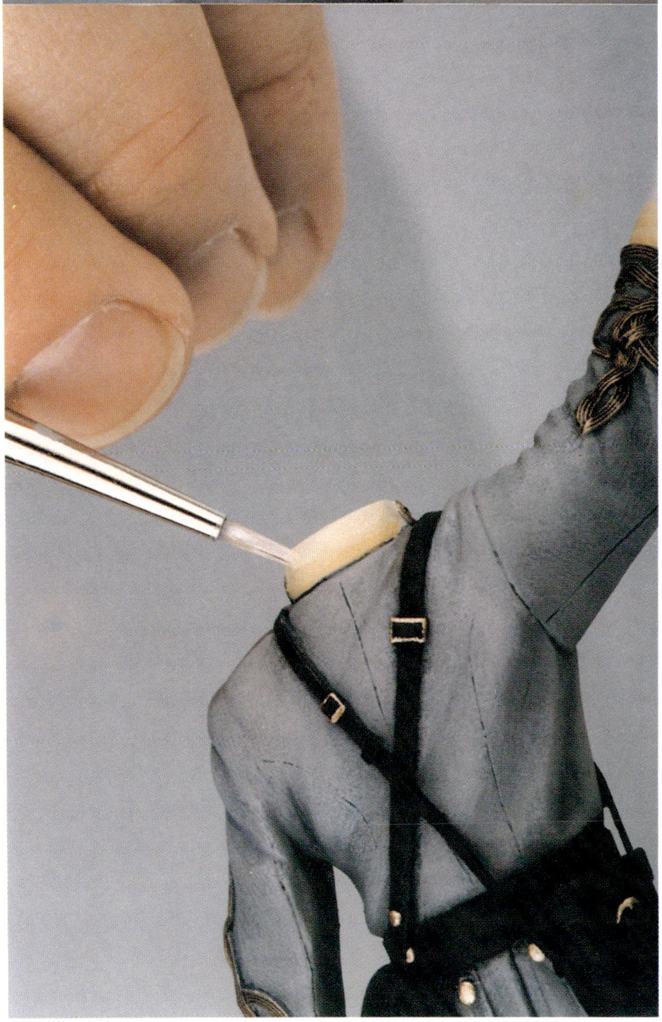

Blend using a dabbing brush motion, feathering the white into your middle color.

The finished collar and cuffs. Also note that I have painted gray on the inside of the collar to insure a shadow effect once the head is glued in place.

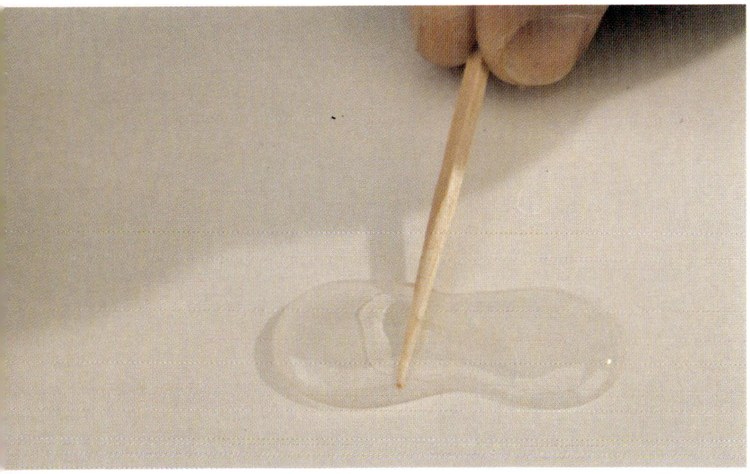

Thoroughly mix equal amounts of epoxy glue to attach the hand and sword. I am using this type of glue to insure a very strong bond.

Make sure you get enough glue on all contact surfaces.

Using a toothpick, carefully apply a small drop into the hole in the arm.

Attach the hand and check for proper alignment.

The hand and sword attached.

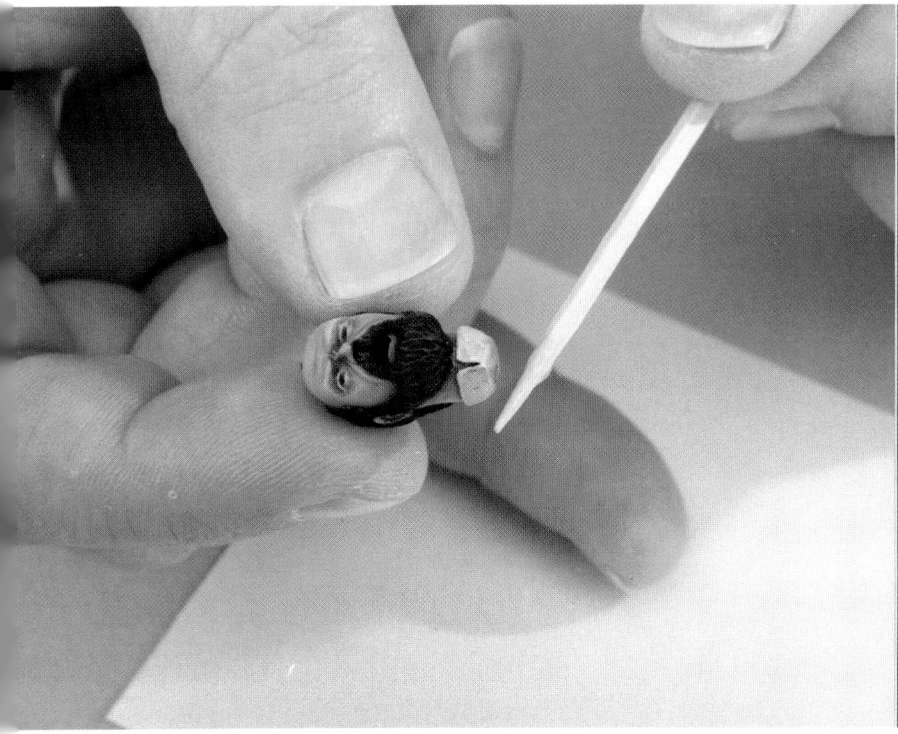

Mix another batch of epoxy glue and apply it to the bottom of the neck.

Attach the head and again check for proper alignment.

The head attached.

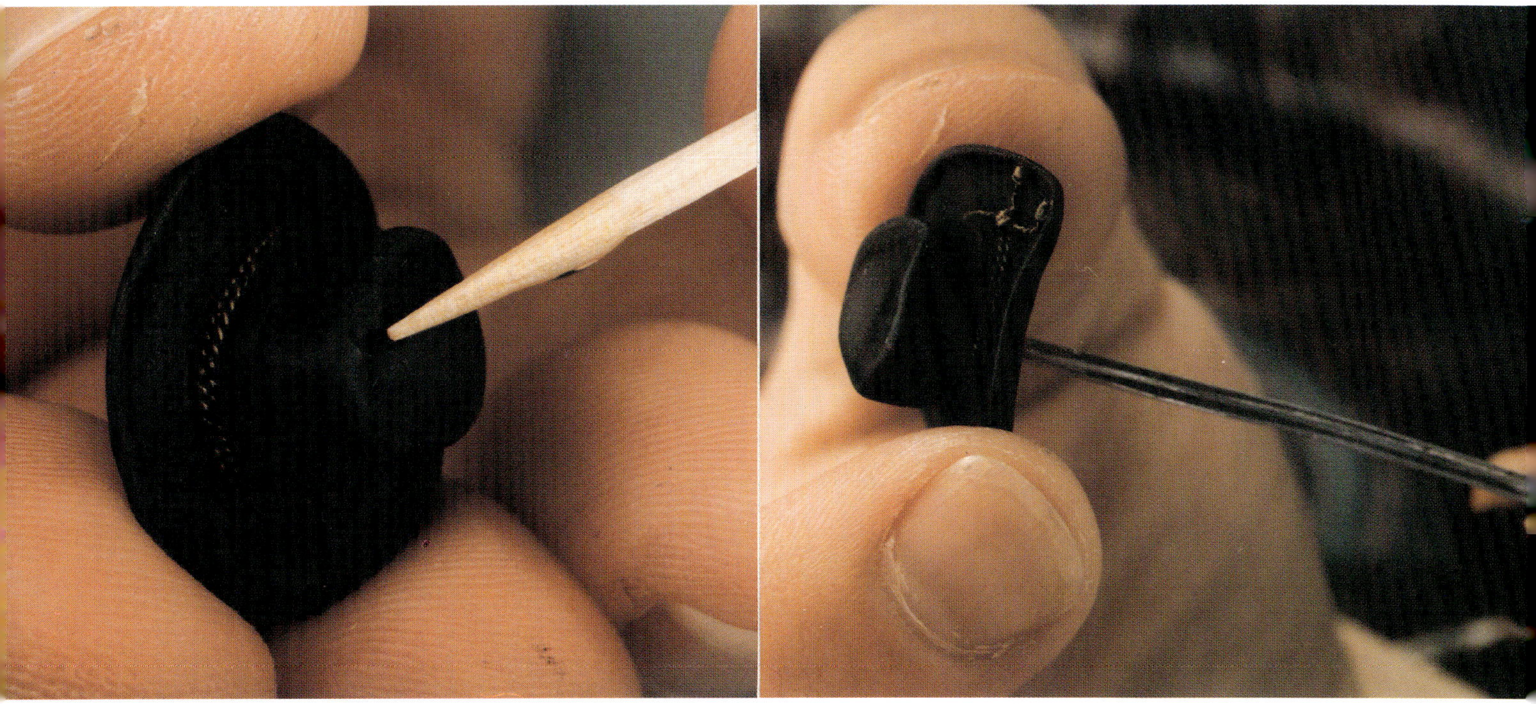

The final item to add is the hat. General Armistead stuck his hat on his sword as he was advancing toward the Union lines. Place a small amount of Super Glue in the slot provided and then slide it down the sword blade. I chose to place the hat about 1/4 of the way down the blade.

Some officers' jackets had piping of the facing color down the front and along the edge of the false flaps on back. The same color that was used for the collar and cuffs needs to be applied. You can mix White hobby paint and Yellow Ocher. You get very good coverage with the hobby paint.

The hat in place on the sword.

Be careful around finished areas.

The finished piping in front.

Like so.

Painting the edges of the false pocket flaps on the back of the jacket.

When you think you are finished, carefully examine the figure and check for any areas that have been missed or where mistakes have been made. Here I am touching up a worn spot on the thumb.

Mixing Civil War Uniform Colors

Federal Dark Blue

The three colors used to mix Federal Blue are Black, Indigo, and White. I mix a small amount of Black with Indigo to create my middle blue, straight Black for the shadow, and using the middle blue I add White for my highlight color.

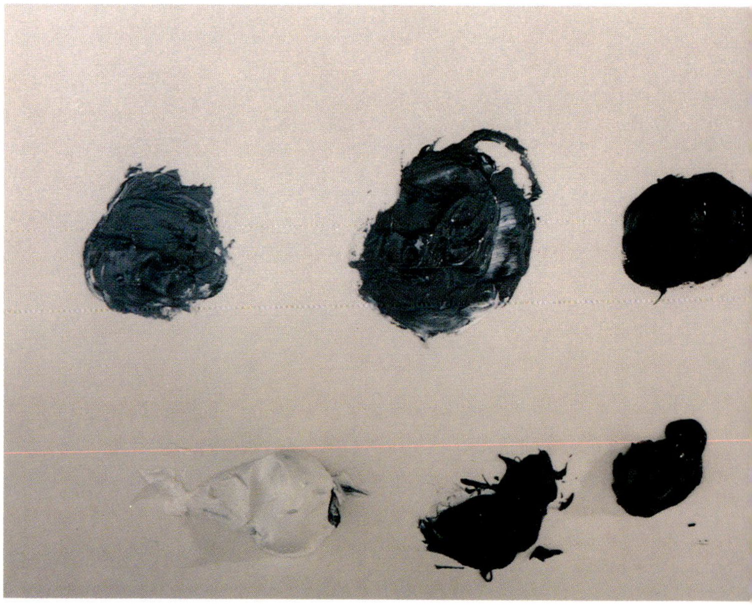

Federal Sky Blue

Federal Sky Blue was, in essence, a lighter version of Federal Dark Blue. I mix Indigo and White together to create my middle color, Indigo and Black together for a shadow, and my middle color mixed with additional White for my highlight.

Confederate Gray

Confederate Gray can be made by mixing Black and White together to produce gray. Black is used as a shadow color; White added to the basic gray is used as a highlight.

Cadet Gray

Cadet Gray is mixed by using Black, White, and Payne's Gray to create a blue-gray middle color. I use Black for the shadow; the middle color mixed with some additional White creates the highlight.

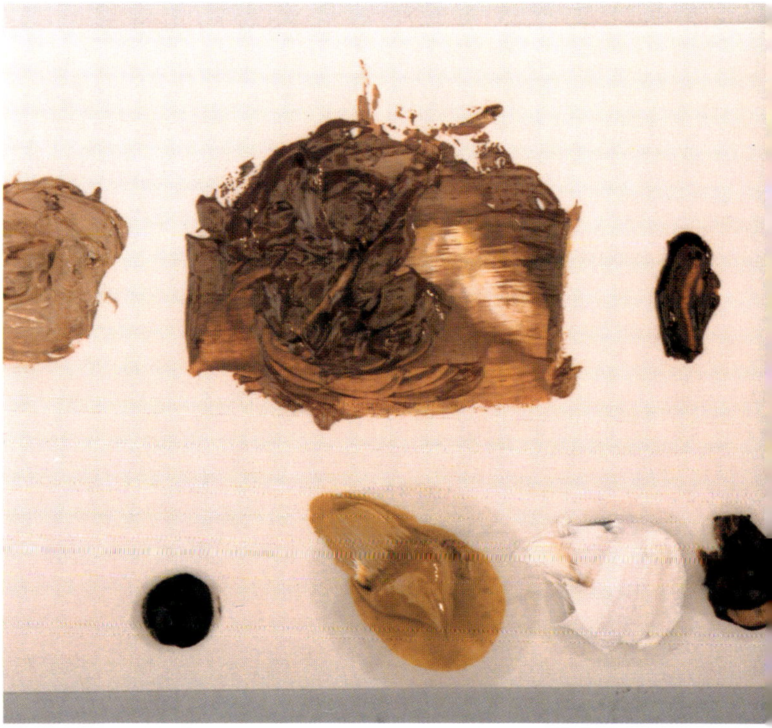

Dark Butternut

Dark Butternut is made combining White, Burnt Sienna, Yellow Ocher, and Burnt Umber. Shadow with Burnt Umber. Highlight is created with the addition of White to the middle color.

Tuscaloosa Gray

This is made by mixing Black, White, and Payne's Gray with a small amount of Yellow Ocher and Raw Umber. This creates a brownish-gray middle color. I shadow with Black; my highlights are created by adding White to the middle color.

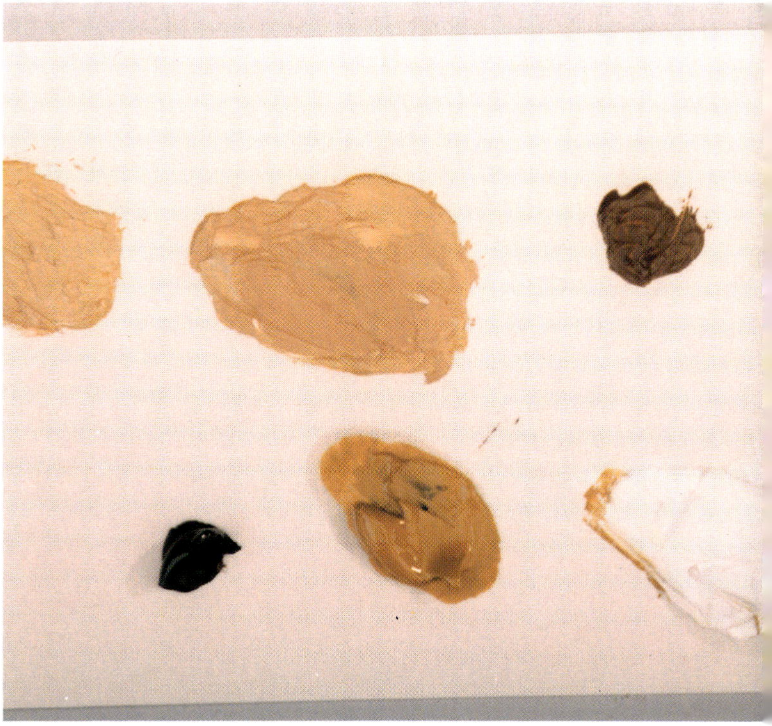

Light Butternut

Light Butternut is made by adding a small amount of Burnt Umber to a mixture of equal amounts of White and Yellow Ocher. My shadow color is Burnt Umber and my light color is a mix of my basic Butternut color and White.

The figure of General Armistead is finished and attached to a wooden pedestal base.

The Gallery

Civil War Federal Infantry

Civil War Confederate Infant